NOTE TO READERS

THIS BOOK TALKS about self-harm and suicide issues. If you are thinking about harming yourself or attempting suicide, tell someone who can help right away. You have many options:

- Go to the nearest hospital emergency room.

- Call emergency services in your area or call, text, or live chat with the Suicide and Crisis Lifeline (https://988lifeline.org/). It provides 24-hour, confidential support to anyone in suicidal crisis or emotional distress.

- Find a therapist or support group in your area.

- July 24th is World Mental Health Day. Samaritans (https://www.samaritans.org/) provides a toolkit with tips on taking care of your own mental health, checking in with others, and raising awareness on social media. Samaritans Awareness Day, held annually on July 24th, emphasises the importance of listening to those going through mental health problems.

Anyone experiencing persistent suicidal thoughts should reach out to a suicide hotline or local emergency number right away.

Dying Into
the Arms of Love

Dying Into
the Arms of Love

A Journey of Love, Loss, & Spirit

Kit Mitchell CCHt, CEG

Professional Evidential Medium, Grief Coach, & Healer
with Over 25 Years of Experience Helping People Find Peace,
Purpose, & Connection Through Spirit Communication

With a Foreword by Laura Davis

Nova & Simon
publishing

Nova & Simon

p u b l i s h i n g

Copyright © 2026 by Kit Mitchell
All rights reserved.
Published by Nova & Simon Publishing
Melbourne, Florida

Although the publisher and the author have made every effort to ensure that the information in this book was correct at press time and while this publication is designed to provide accurate information in regard to the subject matter covered, the publisher and the author assume no responsibility for errors, inaccuracies, omissions, or any other inconsistencies herein and hereby disclaim any liability to any party for any loss, damage, or disruption caused by errors or omissions, whether such errors or omissions result from negligence, accident, or any other cause.

This publication is meant as a source of valuable information for the reader, however it is not meant as a substitute for direct expert assistance. If such level of assistance is required, the services of a competent professional should be sought.

For information about special discounts for bulk purchases or author interviews, appearances, and speaking engagements please contact:

www.KitandNatalie.com

First Edition

ISBN eBook   979-8-9996928-0-1
ISBN Paperback 979-8-9996928-1-8
ISBN Hardcover 979-8-9996928-2-5

Library of Congress Control Number (LCCN): 2025917527

Cover art by Garre Martin
Interior art and flourishes by Bianca Blauth www.pixabay.com/users/6967180/
Edited by Christina DeBusk www.christinamdebusk.com
Design & production by Rodney Miles www.rodneymiles.com

"We're all just walking each other home."

—RAM DASS[i]

To Nova and Simon.

For Rob.

And for Natalie.
Nat, if it weren't for you, I would still be in Derby, and we both know that, and that is not why I married you or moved here to the States.

You will never truly understand how you changed my life, and now I have my first book out. Yes, I know your picture is in it, and your name is on the front and the only bit you wrote was the bit about yourself. But you truly are on each page because of the support you gave me.

You allowed me to be me, even if you don't agree with everything. That Bloody SNU training still getting in my way. Anyway, Nat thank you for all the love and support. —Kit

CONTENTS

FOREWORD

by Laura Davis

"This is not just a book—it's a journey through love,
loss, and what lives beyond"

I'VE KNOWN KIT and Natalie for decades, and I've seen first-hand the extraordinary impact their work and Kit's mediumship has had—not just on my life, but on the lives of countless others I've sent his way. But *Dying Into the Arms of Love?* It's more than a book. It's a portal. It's Kit, in his rawest, realest, most radically generous form, sharing what most won't say out loud and what many of us desperately need to hear.

As someone who's studied shamanic principles and spent years digging into the space between spirit and science, I can say this with deep conviction: The wisdom Kit shares here is a treasure trove. He doesn't just talk about mediumship. He talks about grief, trauma, addiction, God (and not-God), ego, humour, death, healing, humanity. He hands you pieces of his soul, and in doing so, helps you reconnect to yours.

I found myself highlighting entire passages and whispering "YES!" out loud more times than I can count (often with a giggle!). What Kit offers is refreshingly unfiltered and spiritually grounded. There's no ego here, no performance, just a man who has walked through fire, learned many hard lessons, and come out carrying buckets of water for the rest of us.

This book is for the seekers. The sensitives. The sceptics. The grief-stricken. The spiritual-but-not-sure. And it's for anyone who wonders what happens when we die, and how we live more fully because of it.

Dying Into the Arms of Love isn't just Kit's story. It's a hand on your back, guiding you to your own personal truth.

Laura Davis

Founder, Branded Ground
www.BrandedGround.com
Avondale Estates, Georgia
August 2025

PREFACE

FOR A LONG TIME I have been encouraged to write this book. The delay was due to a lack of confidence and belief in myself. My biggest fear was I'd be reinventing the wheel. With so many books out there already on these subjects, what would I say? I didn't want to simply put out bullshit. Ultimately, as mediums and teachers we are tuned in and picking up so much information from the universe, and as this is such a critical time in our growth as a species, after doing mediumship for so long I wanted to write something to help maybe just one person find their own *mediumship* and understand who they are within it. I didn't want the book to be about individual readings or other stuff other mediums write about. I just felt it was the right time to finish off an idea I had twenty years ago, after being called all sorts of dumb names because I was dyslexic.

This is my first book and last. *Oh my God*, I'm not doing this again! (Not true, I've already started books two and three.) It's been fun all the way. The personal stuff hasn't been, but it's been interesting.

So, I am now 65, and I have simply written about my own truths and opinions. I wanted to write something I felt connected too. And here we are, the book finished. You will notice that there are both British and American spelling throughout the book. A bit like me, a mixture of both now. So, while I have a particular sense of humour (I navigate life with it), understand I take my work very seriously. And in these pages, I hope you find at least a part of what you are looking for.

Kit Mitchell

Melbourne, Florida
December 2025

Introduction:

Beyond The Veil

"Death leaves a heartache no one can heal,
love leaves a memory no one can steal."
—Irish Proverb

ARE YOU A medium? Could you be one? Is there a "spirit world?" If so, what does this mean for your worldview? For your healing from loss? For your ability to help others? In a "modern" world where we often hear about a decline in religion, it turns out most people seem to believe in psychic phenomena, in "spirit stuff." In fact a majority of Americans (57%) say they believe in things like extra sensory perception (ESP), telepathy, or experiences they just can't explain away.[ii] And according to a poll of over 1,000 grown-ups, *nearly half* of women surveyed said they've felt the presence of a spirit; *one out of every five of us* has sat with a psychic or medium, and many have had an "otherworldly experience.[iii]"

And while *we are all psychic…* we are not all mediums, even if *you can be.*

"…being a medium and a psychic are two different things that often get lumped together. All mediums are psychic, but not all psychics are mediums. Everyone has psychic ability—the ability to acquire information about the past, present or future. We all have that sixth sense or intuition, that gut feeling when we know something is going to turn out good or bad, like when the phone rings and you know who is calling you before you answer, or that knowing feeling you had that saved you from being in an accident, or by receiving knowledge in your dream state about a certain situation."

—BONNIE PAGE, "Ask the Psychic Medium"[iv]

More on that—much more—in the pages that follow, but you should also know that the psychic business is hot. Over *$2 billion hot.* While other industries go up and down, my line of work has seen steady growth since 2017 and is predicted (not just by psychics) to keep on growing. It seems my home state of Florida has the most mediums anywhere, followed by California, New York, and Texas.[v]

Now, I am definitely not about bragging about industry growth or recruiting people for the money, not at all. I only raise these little facts to show that if you picked up this book for a purpose *you are not alone,* not by a long shot. But when times get tough, when we look into the abyss known as *grief* or suffer from a loss, we tend to then look for answers, for guidance, for comfort.

And it's nothing new. We could look way, way back, and we'll look at more on the history of this stuff soon, but Spiritualism was particularly big before the Civil War, with a higher demand for seances, and there was a surge right through the Great Depression. And when I say you are not alone, I mean it. Kings and queens, business leaders, even modern-day police seek out the help of psychics and mediums.[vi]

Yet in this day and age we mediums seem to be the blunt of even more criticism than the pioneers that paved the way for unfolding and exploration of *Spirit*. And that's just one reason I've written this book. While I *will* explain and warn you, Dear Reader, of the swindles out there, it's simply time to set the record straight. I've been at this a good long while and anyone seeking answers deserves the chance to get them. Too often people are discouraged or scared off from embracing or exploring their gut instincts. This is at the great loss of those who would benefit. And not knowing how to embrace or explore *your abilities* can just as well lead to nowhere, when this doesn't have to be the case.

For much of my early life I tried to ignore my "gifts" because with a family and responsibilities I felt they were more of an intrusion and a curse than a gift. But as time passed, I realized I was able to use these gifts to help others through some of their darkest and lowest times. Today I work—graciously—side-by-side with Spirit. We've come to an understanding and an agreement! There have been so many times that I hated this damn noise in my head. Spirit was talking to me so much that I thought I was crazy. I spent years drinking myself stupid.

But you don't have to do that. In this book I intend to dispel the myths, disabuse you of false ideas and impressions, explain how to explore and develop, and then leave your path where it rightfully needs to be, with *you.*

Being a medium helped me grow on my journey through life, to change my life in a way I never thought possible. In that process, I have been able to help and touch people's lives uniquely and *evidentially*, with the truth that *the love shared with someone here goes on after death.* I have been lucky to find some incredible writers and teachers here and on the other side. I originally named this book *Dying Into Love* after listening to *Becoming Nobody* by Ram Dass. I can tell you that man was incredible. His work is outstanding. He was awesome. He will be remembered for a very long time. He is quoted a few times in this book. One quote in particular is "We're all just dying into love." It is so true, and no matter how many times we've been here, no matter what we have done, good or bad in life here, we are *dying into love.* It's the truth that I have learned from my work: *love is waiting for us all.*

So, what about you? How do people know if they are mediums? One way is through intuitive feelings, gut instincts about people and situations. Other ways are having visions or seeing images that are "not there," hearing voices, feelings of empathy and sensitivity, unexplained experiences, or simply an interest in spirituality. As you'll see, that's how it's happened for me, that and a whole lot of study, training, and practice. *No one can make you a medium but you.* And if you are suffering, perhaps a medium can help.

I was born and grew up (well, that's debatable, as everyone who knows me will say) in England. I took my early training in the Spiritualist Churches of England, Arthur Findlay College and numerous development circles. I've now studied under some of the best mediums in the world. I've also trained as a healer and earned diplomas in anatomy and physiology, body massage, reflexology and nutrition. I became an *evidential* medium (one who provides evidence in a reading that can be confirmed) and psychic in the UK, a Reiki Master, and a teacher in master energy colour healer before I moved to America. I also became a couple's therapist at the University of East London. Then I retrained in the USA as a couples coach, grief coach, and intuitive life coach. I also teach psychic and mediumship development. I have studied under some of the best and worst teachers in the world. I spent years training in the Spiritualist Churches of England, Arthur Findlay College, and numerous development circles, but I learned the most from Rob!

I suppose the question is, do I know what I'm talking about? The answer is sometimes yes and sometimes no. I do not know the truth about death, but you know what? Nobody does. Death is still a great mystery. No one has the answer. Not vicars, priests, preachers, Buddhists, doctors, nurses, or mediums. If you ask anyone, I can tell you no one will have the proper answer. They will have *their* answer, and that's great, but is it yours? We hope and believe that something good is out there waiting for us, and for most of us, that's good enough. If we amalgamate everything from every religion and every belief, there will be just an ounce of truth. My ounce of truth is that I know that, as sure as shit, there is something better out there than this place.

But I became a *trainee medium* the day I was born—*just like you.* Then life chose something different for me and I forgot all about it, perhaps also just like you. I then struggled just to be myself for most of my life, and after being involved in so many different things along the way, I did end up a full-time, working medium, and will always be that *trainee medium* I was born as.

It's been a strange life indeed—experiencing death in everyday circumstances, through my work, and with the passing of family and friends. After the death of my mother, I wasted many years being depressed and angry. And it after enough time had passed, I was shocked to realise I hadn't fully engaged with life, but now that's changed. Now that I'm *living*, I see things more healthily. I face each day, still being a miserable old fart, but I smile, and I try. In fact, I have learnt more *about life from death* than I care to imagine, and the truth is, from death I have learnt who I am. Today I am only truly me when on a platform, being a medium, or doing private readings. Only then am I free and fully engaged with both sides of life and death.

And I have learned that no one is dead, they are just liberated from this place. From my work, I can tell you there is something incredible out there waiting. However, the reality is so much more than we can ever comprehend in the body. But again, that's my truth. What is important is *your truth*. This book is about starting with a thought, taking it to your heart, and finding peace. Some of this information you will know, some will give you a different way to look at it, and some will just make you say, "No, not taking that." If that happens, great. You will have started to find your truth, not mine or any other medium or teacher out there.

This book will not make you a medium, psychic, or a better person. Hopefully, though, I'm helping you open the door to new possibilities. However, with everything in life, it's always up to you to walk through it. But if you do, I can promise you a journey of discovery about who you are that will be second to none. Being a medium is an incredible way to discover so many hidden depths about you, your truth, and your journey into you.

I have written this book for both those questioning if they are or can become a medium, as well as those seeking the guidance and comfort from a medium. I'll share my story, highs and lows, some even lower lows, share what this has taught *me* (your journey is yours). We'll dabble into Spiritualism, so you at least know what you're talking about at parties, explain chakras and auras and other stuff, and then talk directly about both *seeing* a medium and *being* one. And I hope this will be the start of a wonderful *unfolding* of your own path.

But be forewarned, one of the first things people asked when they knew I was going to write a book was if it would be full of swearing! The truth is it *was* full of the F-word, primarily because I was trying to write something that came over as meaningful, funny, and honest— came over as something that could only come from me! But I decided to change it and take them out, leaving only a few in here. And I'm always asked by Americans what this term means, or what that means. They will ask about certain words or phrases they have heard on the telly, so I thought I would give you a little bit of English vocabulary. (Some of the following definitions can be used instead of the word F-word!)

Bollocks. You can also look up the term *ballocks*; they both have the same connotation! So, bollocks is a term for rubbish, often used when someone says something stupid and the reply from someone else who disagreed with them can be, "Oh, what a load of ballocks!" "You're talking ballocks!" Or if you did something wrong, "Oh, bollocks!"

Flipping heck. Flipping heck is often used instead of saying F-ing hell! When I tried to stop swearing, I would often use this expression, but it never really worked out for me!

Sod it. Sod it means forget it; I'll try something else! But it can also mean, let's try it!

Tea. I'm English, so I couldn't write anything without a cup of tea! Drinking tea is probably one of the most important things we do in England; it's what we all love to do. If there's a problem, we have tea. If we're stressed, we have tea. If someone dies, we have tea. It's literally life and death for some of us!

If you sit and have a cup of tea with someone from the UK, you will often hear us say, "You putting the kettle on? I fancy a cuppa," which means I'd like a cup of tea. There are other ways we say this, like everywhere else. We have different dialects from all over the country. If you, or should I say *when* you go to the UK, ask someone to explain how they say TEA!

A brew means to make tea, and it would be put in a question like this, "Do you fancy a brew?" You might hear I fancy a cup of char. If you're in London, you might hear a bit of cockney rhyming slang, which will go like this: "I fancy a cup of rosy Lee," meaning tea. You might hear, "I fancy a builder's brew," which is a cup of robust tea.

Teapots were used to make tea with loose leaves. They're still used, but not as often now. It's now usually made in the cup, with a teabag.

One of the many treats on offer in the UK is high tea, consisting of cucumber or cheese sandwiches and a selection of small cakes. Most of these should be served with jam and cream scones, and you will more than likely use a teapot made with loose tea.

Visitors, be careful of this one, teatime may confuse you in England. We call dinner *dinnertime* in the middle of the day, what the rest of the world calls lunch! Teatime is called teatime for our evening meal, so be careful of that one.

Fancy. Fancy means I like you a lot. It would go in a sentence like this: "You're pretty. I fancy you." And they're probably chatting you up and will have been flirting with you. It generally means that the person is on the pull looking for sex and you are the prey! You may get asked, "Are you up for it?" Be careful; they're asking you for sex! Fancy could also be when something looks fancy, like a fancy piece of furniture, or "Do you fancy a cup of tea?" meaning, do you want a cup of tea?

Fortnight. When I first got to America, I would say this a lot. "See you in a fortnight," which means see you in two weeks.

Mum. Mother.

Mam. Also *mother,* but what I called my step-mum. Some say it's short for "ma'am."

Pissed. When I'm out with friends in the USA, I have often said, "God, I'm pissed," which gets the answer,

"Who with?" When you're pissed in the UK, it means you're drunk. You might also hear, "I'm plastered, wrecked, out of my brain." You may even hear one of us say, "Don't fall arse-over-tit," which means don't fall over.

Telly. You will often hear us say, "What's on the telly tonight?" or, "Did you watch that program on the telly last night?" Ok, telly is just a short word for television.

"May your God go with you."

—DAVE ALLEN, comedian

"To live in hearts we leave behind is not to die."

—THOMAS CAMPBELL

"Grief is the last act of love we can give to those we loved. Where there is deep grief, there was great love."

—EARL GROLLMAN

"They that love beyond the world cannot be separated by it. Death cannot kill what never dies."

—WILLIAM PENN

"Your passed loved ones are not dead and gone... They are with you every single day, and they aren't missing out on what's happening in your life, either."

—RORY WALKOM

Part I:

Confessions Of A Lifelong Medium

CHAPTER 1:

MY CONNECTION TO SPIRIT...
OR *WEIRDNESS*.

THOUGH I GO by Kit, my full name is Kitione—*Reverend Kitione "Kit" Mitchell*, actually—evidential medium, intuitive coach, spiritual healer, and Reiki Master. I was born in 1960 in (the Isle of) Portland, Dorset, which has been called "ruggedly beautiful," and raised in Derby, England, known as one of England's "most haunted" cities, where "The city's historic cathedral quarter serves as the gateway to the Peak District National Park, where rolling hills, babbling brooks, and traditional country pubs are reminiscent of a Romantic painting." In truth, I'm no different than you, and my life hasn't been that bad, I'm just a little stranger than most.

My first decade in this place (the 1960s) saw the Civil Rights Movement, the escalation of the war in Vietnam, and the Space Race between the USA and Soviet Union. But it also saw the rise of youth culture, rock and roll, social change, like the birth control pill. And in 1964 my parents divorced when I was four. I then lived with my mother, Pauline, and brother, Kevin, until I was seven, when my journey through pain and fear started the night my mother died.

I have no memory of this or the time she died. I only remember Kevin and me in bed with her the following day. Kevin was bouncing up and down, trying to wake her up, and a lady from across the street came over and wanted to know, "Where are the towels?" Strange, the things we remember. Many years later, my first wife, Trudy, and I found out by getting the coroner's report that my mum had died sometime during the night—or as we like to say now, *passed over into the light*—of an *ectopic pregnancy* (a pregnancy that happens outside of the uterus).

She died and left us, and I can tell you that even today at 65, it is still painful.

Six months later, my connection to *Spirit* or *weirdness* began when Mum appeared as a big bright light at the bottom of the bed, scaring the crap out of me. At seven and a half, I pulled the sheets over my head and started to scream with no sound coming out of my mouth as I saw her *light* walking up the side of the bed through the covers. She then leaned over, kissed me on the head, and left. *Thanks, Mum!* That was the beginning of my weird journey.

After that my brother Kevin and I went to live with our dad, George, and Mam Anne (stepmother), and our two half-brothers, Nicky and Gary. Neil was born later that year, making five boys. For all the pain and trouble we went through as a family, we remain very much that to this day—*a family*. I grew up as the eldest of five brothers, and all of us were good Christians. We went to Sunday School, Boys

Brigade, and the Christian Youth Club. Oh, boy, was I God-fearing! I believed in the Bible but was confused by its strange message. But what the hell did I know as a child?

My mam (Anne) told me that when I was thirteen, I went completely strange. The truth is I became a complete bastard! Having hormones, psychic stuff in my head, and emotions flooding my body, to say I was weird would be an understatement. I suppose I went through the teens as normally as possible but always knew something was wrong. A raging hormonal psycho with psychotic and psychic tendencies? That's normal, right?

I started work at thirteen, window cleaning and a paper round (delivering newspapers). I was a kid who liked buying my own clothes and records. However, when I left school and went to work, all I ever got told by the old farts I worked with were things like:

"We fought in a war for you."

"Get your hair cut."

"We fought for you to have the freedom that you take for granted."

Well, I'm sorry, and thank you, but if Hitler were around today, I would fight him!

The real problem was that everyone had their place. If you went to school and did well, you would succeed. You would get all the things your parents wanted and could never have. If you didn't do well, you would be a waste of space and time! And I was always in trouble at school—fighting, wrecking classrooms, fighting again, or stealing milk (my dad's favourite story to tell people). I ran away from home a couple of times, and I tried suicide a couple of times. Once, I took a bottle of aspirin; another time I was going to jump off a bridge… Again, it's usual stuff for a teenager, right? I got in trouble with the police, at school, and with my parents, and yes, I created it!

17

When you are a big family and everyone is doing their own thing, you don't always get the help you need. We were all looking for attention in our own way, good or bad. It was no one's fault. Everyone had to work, and it wasn't easy having a family, let alone five boys, to bring up. Our parents deserve medals! So, like most teenagers, I was not too fond of the world and would not allow anything or anyone to hurt me again. I constantly lashed out at life and anyone in the way. The reality was that I was scared, and when I look back at it, I see this little boy lost and alone.

My first job was at the Derbyshire Royal Infirmary, the main hospital in Derby. By the age of 15, I had been on a school volunteer course once a week, and over the Christmas period I asked if I could help. My willingness got me a job offer as a porter. Then, I became a plaster technician in the orthopaedics department, working with two crazies, Cyril and Ricky. They were both great friends, but both have passed. And when I left school at sixteen, I left with a degree in painting toilets black. Yes, that is literally what we did. Because we weren't sitting for exams, we painted toilets—me, Ade Williams, and Ray Colbourn. Over the next couple of years, I settled into work, making enough money to buy the stuff that was important to me: *clothes*. I bought expensive new shirts most weeks, even had made-to-measure suits. I looked like a right-bobby dazzler!

At seventeen I left home. I was *trying to grow*, as young people do, and my parents tried to stop that. So, I went to live at Cyril's house (my friend from my plaster technician days). I was supposed to get my own flat at some point, but that didn't happen because I was staying rent-free, so I ended up sleeping on his couch. I suppose this was where the drinking all started. I drank most nights, went to the pub, went to the chip shop (British fast food, mostly fried), came home, went to sleep, got up, and went to work. I was working, and I was drinking. I bought a motorbike and spent more time on the road lying on my back than riding it, always falling or getting knocked off.

Eventually, I had a massive argument with Cyril. He was trying to get me to grow up. I was a young kid and stupid. I thought I knew how to be a man. Hell, I was drinking like one in the pub. *It's what everyone else does.* I felt that Cyril was trying to do the same thing as my parents: control me. And as the saying goes, "Trying to put an old head on young shoulders" never fucking works.

University was for the rich, and the rest of us were going to work until we dropped dead or retired, and then dropped dead. It was this way for years. There was nothing to live for and that's how I saw it as a kid. As I watched my parents getting older, it was reinforced. Life was boring. I went to work, slept, and went out a couple of times a week. And if I made money, I would go to the pub and drink, drink, drink!

Then, I had a bit of a meltdown at eighteen.

It was at this point I met Trudy, my first wife, at Tiffany's, a nightclub in Derby. As all of this was going off with Cyril, Trudy and I ran away to the seaside town of Skegness. It's a tiny coastal resort in the UK (picture Atlantic City). I worked on the fairground, the dodgem cars, and then on to mock auctions. Next, I went to Birmingham in the West Midlands, lived there for a year, and eventually returned to Derby (for the next 30 years.) In Birmingham, our first child, Nova, was born in 1979. Then we went back to Skegness for a few months, and then a complete turnaround, returning to Derby in the East Midlands. We married two years later, and our second child, Simon, was born in 1981.

I worked in factories for another six years and returned to the hospital in the Accident and Emergencies Department for the next seven years. Life went on from there, and I worked 60 or 70 hours a week to make ends meet. It didn't change for most of my life. That's just how it was. I would work, make money, eat, drink, and sleep! Don't get me wrong, I had a family, tried to be a good dad and be there for them, but at that time, when you were young and needed the money, you worked.

I felt like I had let everyone down for years. I felt like I let my parents down and, worse, Trudy, Nova, and Simon—my own family. Not listening at school and not getting the education I should have, I had trapped everyone, and they deserved better! That's how I saw my life, that *I was to blame*.

It was all so dreary and dull. It felt like it was going to go on forever. *Oh my God*, I was trying not to be in this system. I fought everything and everyone! But in the end—yes, you got it—I became a part of it. I binge drank once a week. Then, as time went on, two nights a week. I had to fight everything and everyone for years. I felt if I surrendered, I would lose everything. I lived in fear. I had to keep moving. I went from job to job, never making much money, just enough for us to get by, but that was it. I knew I could do much more but was always too scared I wouldn't be good enough or I would fail. I hated everything so much that I couldn't do anything better for myself. If I tried and lost, then I was open to all sorts of crap running around my head about failure. *What would happen to my marriage or my kids? Would I lose everything?*

So, I simply kept going, hating everything more and more. I lost the will to move forward because I couldn't trust. In my head, there would always be another shitload of bad things happening that I didn't want because of the shit I'd already been through. It was like playing catch twenty-two: you were screwed if you did and screwed if you didn't.

Eventually, my friend Audrey Norris gave me a chance to act in the revue (theatre), which helped me realise I could do other things. (*Thank you, Audrey xx.*) So, I left the hospital again, this time to be an actor. I went to the local college, walked into a room where a band was practising, started singing, and the next thing, they asked me to join. *Hmmm*, was I shocked that I could sing!

In 1983 our lives changed in one month. Trudy's mum, my mother-in-law, Joan, died. She was a truly lovely lady. And then my best friend Cyril's mum died, a real lady in every sense of the word. Both passed within three weeks of each other. I think this was the first kick in my armour. These women were like mothers to me and losing them both in such a short period really hurt. And as I had never mourned out loud as a child, it was my first experience with grief. I had no idea how I kept working. And again, being "the man," I did not get help; *it's not what one did.*

Then, my life would be changed forever. Trudy said one day, "We are going to the Spiritualist Church."

"You can," I said, "but no, I'm not going in there." After all, that was *evil*, and I was sorry, but I could not go against my religious beliefs. Even though I had weird stuff going on, at twenty-three, I was still a God-fearing little boy, being a bit impetuous and young. I remember clearly saying, "Flipping heck, I am a Christian and do not agree with that stuff!"

Yet one night, during the deepest, darkest night in the UK that year, we crossed the threshold into damnation and hell, and the lights started to flicker… My head spun around, and I threw up pea-green soup! Okay, maybe that didn't happen, but that is how some people would see it as we walked into a *Spiritualist Church* (the Spiritualist Church in Charnwood St. Derby). As a good Christian boy, I suppose that alone would get us banished from heaven, if I was still a good Christian boy.

Chapter 2:

If I Could Become a Medium…

THE REALITY OF the night was, it was a warm summer evening, and, to our amazement, these people were *normal*. Hmmm, well, most of them were! I was very sceptical and, honestly, that has never changed. (I am English; it is what we do well.) We met a couple of people who would become guides, teachers, and good friends for life, namely Ida Harrison and Pat Collett. Pat was learning to be a medium, and we would become close friends. They are both still a part of my work today. As a teacher, I often tell people how Ida explained things clearly, and Pat helped me with other stuff.

On the first night in church, we had extraordinary evidence of survival from Joan, my mother-in-law, and then Cyril's mum. Finally,

I was given my mother. To say I was shocked was an understatement! Trudy and I felt we had found our way home. We went back week-after-week, learning while getting messages from our loved ones' grandmas, granddads, aunts, friends, and old work colleagues.

I was given the name of a medium who did one-on-one sittings and booked a private reading. She was one of Derby's most gifted spiritual mediums, and she was another true lady and unbelievable human being, Eva (Evelyn) Carrington. Eva became a friend, teacher, and lifesaver. She changed my direction in life, which changed the person I was. Ultimately, she was one of the driving forces behind my becoming the medium I am today. Eva passed away a few years ago, and I miss her dearly. However, lucky for me, I still feel her presence when working. I will arrive at a church, and they will have picked her favourite hymn. I have never told anyone what it is, but it is always on the list when she is around. (*Thank you, Eva xx.*)

I remember attending a Sunday night *divine service*[1], where I witnessed a medium on the platform for the first time. I listened to her philosophy and thought, *Wow, mediums have all the answers. I want to be one! If I could become a medium, I would understand what this life was all about and help others.*

Our visits continued and education flowed into my body and brain. I was still attending the Thursday night open circle, trying different services, and watching different mediums work. I loved it. The more I saw, the more I wanted to learn. I would become a medium to

---

[1] A Spiritualist church's Sunday night divine service is a community gathering that combines inspirational talks and spiritual philosophy with the demonstration of mediumship, where a medium relays messages from the spirit world. The service typically includes uplifting music, prayers (including a healing prayer), an inspirational address, and a closing. Many services are open to everyone, regardless of background or belief, and often conclude with a social gathering with refreshments.
—Google AI Overview, accessed 12/3/25

find the spiritual answers to life. I became a therapist and coach to see and heal the psychological side of (my) life. I am still looking at both, as my friend Rob and a few others, including Spirit, have pointed out, I am a slow learner! But I started medium work because I wanted to help people.

Spiritualism was a significant movement in 1983, when I walked through the doors. It wasn't all about awards, badges, and ego. It was about kindness and for the most part, still is today. And I was so lucky to have met older mediums from the Spiritualist movement. They did their work with love and understanding. Sure, there were always odd ones that were using it for gain, but for the most, these kind people did it from their hearts.

The teachers and friends I met at this church were a great help, and their friendship will last a lifetime. I eventually became a member of the Spiritualist National Union (SNU) after many years of going in and out, all thanks to my friend Pat. I was welcomed into the church by the visiting medium of the day, Mavis Pattilla. I don't think she remembered it, but she shook my hand (not the *throat*, the *hand!*) and gave an excellent little speech. For the next few years, Trudy and I became addicted to learning about being mediums and healers.

CHAPTER 3:

WE ARE NEVER ALONE

IN 1987 I started singing in rock bands. The best six months were spent with Juler who was brilliant, as the Nozie Boys—him on guitar and me with a tambourine, having a laugh. I turned professional from 1992 to 2010, singing in pubs, clubs, and holiday camps throughout England, at first with my mate Duncan. We were a duo called The Mitchell Express. After a few years, I went out doing more of the same on my own with backing tracks and met some great agents like Kim Holmes from Showbiz Entertainment, a great guy.

As time went on, Trudy and I became a little disillusioned with all the politics and BS that goes with any church. We went back into our Spiritualist Church in Charnwood and then stopped again. A few things happened with other people playing power games, taking over the church, and running it their way. It is always the way. I like to call it the *human element*. It gets involved, and sometimes, as we like to say, a new broom will sweep clean. Hmmm, famous last words!

Over the 12 years since we found the church, I dropped in occasionally, still meeting up with Pat. She was going far with her mediumship. After a while, I developed my own. Although I was still trying to find a teacher I could trust, I'd attend classes here and there, but to no avail. I could not find the one to set me on my way! Over the years, I also read books by Doris Stokes and other well-known mediums from the 1980s and earlier, looking for inspiration. Time moved on into the 1990s and Trudy went to university. During her first year, I went into a complete shutdown and then an overdrive of emotions. I felt like I was being left again.

I went into that little boy mode and struggled with everything. But this time, *my wife was leaving me*. I started going through my life crisis at thirty-seven, first because Trudy went to college and then due to empty nest syndrome. My son Simon joined the Royal Air Force, and my daughter Nova got ready to leave home with her future husband, Kevin. I imploded over the next four years. I just lost myself in pain and loneliness. It really was no one's fault, and I would never blame anyone. It's what happens when the universe comes calling and telling you *it's time to do what you're here to do*.

Despite being petrified, I decided to do something about myself. I pushed myself to attend college, where I completed the Foundations in Education. It was also counted as my first year of four at university. During this first year, I was given the phone number of Mrs. Heather of the Learn Write Centre in Long Eaton, UK, and someone finally realised I was dyslexic. I had to learn to write from the start, which was not fun, but I developed better handwriting.

So, after leaving school at 16 with an exceptional degree in toilet painting, I was now getting an education at 38. I can tell you it is no joke. It was hard at times, and I did not get everything right, but I was doing something I was told I could never do. I was proving I was not thick or stupid. Better still, I showed everyone I could amount to *anything*—not the opposite. No more toilet painting for me! At college, I studied English Literature and History. It was great, and I finally believed I could do something more. I did assignments, read books, and went to lectures. Trudy sat with me to ensure I was going in the right direction, pushing and encouraging me along with Nova and Simon. If not for her helping me, I would never have gotten that far. I triumphantly finished my first year and promptly took six months out. God, I was stressed!

I eventually returned to college, earning diplomas in anatomy, physiology, body massage, reflexology, and nutrition. After I finished, I started back in September to do aromatherapy but left before I passed because Trudy and I split. The next three years were unpleasant with the divorce. And dearest reader, I don't think I need to go through this bit. Divorce is divorce. It's all BS—*he said, she said*—we all know the truth. It's all about perception. Nobody wins. It's painful for everyone involved. Most of us get the picture, and if you have not been through this, count yourself lucky!

As my personal life was falling apart, I went back into the church and started receiving healing. I turned to Spirit and finally asked for help. I returned home and was welcomed by my guides and helpers. Although they never left me, I felt that through those four years I had been deserted. However, it was a good lesson that *we are never alone*. My favourite poem is "Footsteps in the Sand" by Margaret Fishback Powers. If you are lonely or think you have been deserted, give it a read.

29

"My son, my precious child,
I love you and I would never leave you.
During your times of trial and suffering,
when you see only one set of footprints,
it was then that I carried you."

—from "Footprints" by MARGARET FISHBACK
POWERS

I threw myself back into the church and trained as a healer but never finished because of the politics (again) in the church. And after going through the usual things people do when becoming single again (nudge, nudge, wink, wink!), I met Manj in the first year after my split. We became great friends first, then we fell in love. She gave me something, and she believed in me *differently*. Although I had been playing around with my spiritual work since 1983, it wasn't until 2004 that I decided to work professionally as a medium. That was due to the encouragement I received from Manj.

A couple of years later, I became a counsellor. I became a couples' therapist mainly because of the counselling I received during my divorce. Margaret Slater and Anthony E. Hartwell were amazing therapists. This support pushed me to return to the University of East London. *I finally got there. I achieved something through education.* I became a relationship counsellor, where I focused on counselling couples and individuals on relationship issues. It had all changed. I was living in my new world after becoming a counsellor. I now had new skills to use.

Next, I became a support worker (again with Manj's help) in Nottinghamshire, then Derby and Derbyshire, supporting people with addiction. I worked at Mansfield District Council, Phoenix Futures, and Action Housing, to name a few.

Okay, I'll point this out: I was helping people with the same problem. I was an alcoholic. It's just who I was (am), but I hid it like we all do. I loved my work and was blessed to meet some great people, clients, and colleagues. The one great friend and colleague, Sharon, was just one of God's own. And the advice to everyone was not to mess with her! Oh, and my favourite bit, she swore way worse than me. Sharon died in Nottingham while working on the streets as an outreach worker. She was helping people she so cared for, and her death was a significant loss to everyone who knew her, especially me. She was a great friend. I miss her to this day.

During this time, my relationship with Manj was constantly up and down. We finally broke up. The day she moved into her new apartment was painful for us both. We tried couples therapy three times and were at the end. As a friend, Marian Hope Clarke, said, "We couldn't live with each other but couldn't live without each other." That was so true at the time! We had been a significant force in each other's lives and healed a lot, but it didn't work. I'm happy she's happy now. We speak occasionally and she tells me she smokes cigars and drinks whiskey now and has a new life.

Interlude:

A Note From My Wife, Natalie

I TOOK A different path to finding my goals in life. I lived the eat, pray, love life all on my own, then found myself back at the beginning — or, as I like to call it, "back at the bottom of the pile!" This is good for people to understand as this journey continues to this day!

Spiritual work is filled with many people with varied backgrounds, and I am no different. I began my career in the corporate world in advertising and marketing over thirty-plus years ago. As an executive, I experienced a fast-paced work environment and truly understand the need to balance work and personal life.

I have been fortunate to work worldwide and experience many different cultures and environments. When faced with a fork in the road, I took the following steps down a path that unfolded in an amazing direction; I learned to ask not what I wanted to do but what wanted me. And what wanted me was the spiritual path.

I started my spiritual journey in 2005, completely immersing myself in training, reading countless books, and taking many courses and lectures in the USA. But I knew I had to do more to fulfil my dreams and soul purpose. I quit my corporate job as a Director of Marketing and relocated to the UK, where I began training at Arthur Findlay College (AFC), the College of Psychic Studies in London, and sitting in weekly development circles at Spiritualist Churches and privately throughout the UK.

While developing and attending AFC, I discovered other gifts I was blessed with, such as the ability to do trance and spiritual portraits of loved ones who have passed. At that time, I also started attending Coach U's Advanced Life Coaching Program, which I subsequently finished in December of 2012.

In one of my many courses at AFC with world-renowned medium Colin Bates, Spirit took my life in another direction, one I did not even think would happen. They introduced me to my future husband, Kit. I went to the UK repeatedly, I guess, because I was supposed to meet Kit. And all my dreams (or nightmares) came true. I married him! (If you are reading this, Simon, I am still held under the floorboards.)

Chapter 4:

Lost & Found

I DECIDED TO find the right teacher and return to my mediumship. I had known how to work as a medium for a long time, but like most people who enter this field of work, I suffered from extremely low self-esteem and a lack of belief in myself. Time went on, and a few years later, on one strange Sunday, I went to Belper Spiritualist Church in a town in Derbyshire. The medium working that day was Mr. Robert Brown. Now, talk about strange: he worked in the same building I worked out of in Nottingham. Hmm. Spirit has a fabulous way of doing things!

After a conversation, Rob invited me into his circle[2] and I started working again. He encouraged me to go for it in many ways, from going to Arthur Findley College (where I met Natalie) to working in psychic suppers. Psychic suppers are nights where several mediums work and then they give you food afterwards. I finally found my teacher, someone I could trust and believe in.

When I went to Stanstead, I was blessed to meet three more great teachers: Colin Bates, Sadie Baker, and Angie Morris. But in truth, Rob was not only my teacher and best friend, he had also become a total inspiration to me.

In 2011, my new wife Natalie and I became the tenth and eleventh accredited teachers worldwide of an amazing new healing technique known as Master Energy Colour Healing. The healing uses colour and sound poured down from the ascended masters and archangels. It has a much finer, purer vibration, and the colours used are much paler and more luminous than any colours used before.

Then in March of 2015 I completed the Core Essentials Program from Coach U.

And at last… a few years ago, I stopped drinking and realised that I was (I am) an alcoholic. It all ended in May of 2017, and I was fortunate. I was helped by an incredible lady and friend, Judith. She became my rock through a very trying time.

Today I am one lucky person, taking one for England and living in the USA. Well, someone has to! Since getting here, I have travelled

---

[2] A development or open circle in mediumship is a supportive, structured group session where people of all levels (beginners to experienced) gather to practice and enhance their psychic and mediumship abilities in a safe, non-judgmental space, often led by an experienced medium. Participants meditate, share spiritual insights, practice giving and receiving messages from spirit, learn techniques, and connect with a like-minded community to grow their connection to the spirit world.

across America, bringing my brand of mediumship to the good old folks. And yes, I can hear everyone who knows me in the UK groaning, "Poor Americans!" I'm meeting some incredibly talented individuals, young and old. I am trying to give them an understanding that will enable them to take their personal lives and mediumship to new heights.

My trips and work in the USA have been great so far. I've visited 27 states and worked in nine, and I plan to do more. It all started with a trip to Connecticut with friends Sage and Colleen, the other two Americans we met at Arthur Findley Collage. Then, we went to Boston with Lori Doupe, Los Angeles with Ami Manning, our TV manager, and Doylestown in Philadelphia with Susan Duval.

Susan got us an interview with Eric Anzalone, the biker from the Village People. He has a TV show called *What Matters Most*. It was an incredible experience meeting him and everyone associated with the program. This came out of the blue during our first year of working here. We weren't even scheduled to do this. Other mediums from the UK had visa troubles, and through our friend Nan Falk, who knew Susan Duval, we were asked to fill in at the last minute.

I have also worked in New York. Nat's friends arranged a couple of nights' work on Long Island and New Jersey. Then, we visited Atlanta with Laura and Arlington in Washington with Reverend Nancy and Witney. I have worked all over Florida, where I live now, with Nat, including Kissimmee and Melbourne, in the Spiritualist Church with Emma.

I have worked in Jacksonville with Caroline Sznakowski and Alex Gamel in Jax Beach. And as Rob liked to say, "It's not bad for a scruffy kid from Derby!" Nat and I took Rob on several of these trips, which neither of us ever believed we would accomplish in this life. I owe many thanks to people throughout my travels in the USA, including Spirit. I continue to meet great people wherever I go, and now I'm a citizen, something I achieved in 2018. So, I can call them my fellow Americans. Natalie and I were regularly doing church services, psychic suppers/circles, public demonstrations, one-to-one readings, healing sessions and workshops both here in the States as well as abroad. Along the way I enrolled in the Advanced Coaching program.

It's been eight years now, and I would be a liar if I told you that I didn't miss a drink. I do. Sometimes, the stress of who I am and what I do gets to me. No different than anyone else. The truth of what I am, though, is I'm an addict, plain and simple! To drink again would be the worst thing I could ever do. Judith encouraged me to go to the 12-step program meetings, and I still participate in them from time to time today.

When I started drinking, it helped my head relax and helped me shut down, it did for quite a while. Then, it started to get worse because I was so unhappy with what was happening in my personal life. I finally realised that enough was enough after waking up on a bench by the Tampa Bay shore at four in the morning after having a massive argument with Nat. I was drunk. I had consumed five pints of beer, half a bottle of wine, and about eight shots of whiskey. I cannot remember much after that. Leading up to this night, I drank wine, beer, and whisky every night for quite a while. I was tired and lonely, living a life I wasn't happy doing. But after that night, I realised I had to change, and I did.

I am now clean, and I can promise you it is very painful looking at what I have done over the years due to drinking myself into oblivion. In my twenties, I played with drugs. The word is "experimented" (!) but alcohol was the bigger problem. Nevertheless, I'm sober now, and every day I'm *doing it*. It is not easy. My friend Judith has helped and has been honest with me. She is my counsel, guide, and teacher. Through her, I have found my way. I know that I cannot drink anymore (being a former drug and alcohol support worker in my forties, I knew what I had to do). It took me a long time to face the truth about what I was like with a drink!

I now know, being sober, I'm one of the luckiest people alive. I followed a dream: I live in Florida in the good old US of A, and I have my hair, teeth, and a body that works (hmm, *just*). My back is wrecked because I was rear-ended twice at traffic lights, but apart from that, I'm breathing... I'm alive. And here in America, I am helping people become their authentic selves, and let me tell you, I'm incredibly proud of the work I do. I'm very privileged to have met some fantastic people who have sought me out for medium readings and to get some help from both sides of the veil called death. Now, as a grief coach and hypnotherapist, I can help people in many ways. Maybe that's all my journey has been about: assisting others to come to terms with themselves and the love that has gone on before.

But it's what I do.

Part II:

The Biggest Lesson
In The Universe

MY FEELINGS OR questions about this place (Earth) are not that strange from anyone else's. For example, I have to question who would create a place with so much hurt and pain. Whether we realise it or not, *we* did. We all contribute to the whole movement on Earth. The main problem now is bringing destruction to something that has just been loaned to us. This place will probably be taken away from us at some point, and we will have to be moved somewhere else. The souls that have finished their journeys will come back as Spirits and restore the Earth to its glory for every other species except us humans!

I always had the feeling that it was all set up so wrong. Who would allow abuse of every kind to be inflicted on us as humans, let alone the animals, trees, Earth, oceans, and anything else we as the human race deem below us? Again, the answer is pretty straightforward: we do! The age-old question is, *Why doesn't God step in?* Simple: Why should he? We are supposedly at the top of the food chain, and again, supposedly, we're the clever ones! We breathe and question everything, and yes, we think we know all there is to know. Obviously, we don't. Truth is, we are born and everyone else controls us. There's so much more I want to say here but it will just sound bitter and political. We are always saying we are free, that we live in a free world. In reality, we're not. What is the honest answer to all of this? It turns out that this place is set up correctly. Again, not by God but by us!

We agree to an adventure into life and the possibilities of change within us. We come here to experience things fully. We do pick most of the stuff that happens to us, but we do it for ourselves—not for God, but in an attempt to be of service to each other. Then, if you're like me, we bitch and moan that it's not fair. (Just so you know, I'm one of life's biggest bitchers. I'm always moaning about something!) But I have a set amount of time to learn stuff before I go back up there and be set free! Hmm, yeah right...not! Like most of us, I have to come back again and again and again to clean up my stuff.

To put it into perspective, this time in this life, I *chose* to be a son, brother, father, granddad, and husband two and a half times. I also chose to be a friend, hypnotherapist, coach, teacher, medium, psychic, healer, and teacher of meditation and hypnotherapy. As well, in the process, a major pain in the arse, idiot, and alcoholic—and I've managed to fit in all these over the space of sixty-five years! Sometimes, I am nice, a friend, someone who inspires people to live. So, not bad for a human being. Could I be more? Yes. Could I do more? Yes. I could but that's down to me and my choices.

It's my life and I will decide what I want to be as I grow older (or grow up) as long as I contribute in my own way. I will find some small peace; I try and do my bit. Am I sitting on Greenpeace's Rainbow Warrior? No. But I contribute when possible. I could always do more, like most.

This book's original title was going to be *LIFE: An Adventure into Love,* because we take this journey every time we are born. We put a new shell on. We start a new life, create a new personality, and live a life to gain new experiences. There's no big secret to life. It's just an introduction to love. That's all it's about. Nothing else. The absolute truth about love is that it has to doubt, disbelieve, hate, and fight everything before it can find its truth. We must go through everything, every piece of hell you could imagine. Each soul goes through this, and life will not end here for any soul until the work is done and that soul releases itself. This won't happen until it has passed the true goals it set at the beginning of the journey.

There's no big secret to life. It's just an introduction
to love. That's all it's about. Nothing else.

When we come here, each time we set specific goals, our soul will make some kind of progress, no matter what it does. Some of us are lucky and will learn quite quickly. Some won't, but that is not held against you. Once that's complete and the soul can't grow anymore in the body, it goes out to do work as a guide. When that's done, it's onto the next bit. Just know that you are part of a universe that wants you to continue to grow and grow beyond anything the brain could ever fathom.

Each time we come here, we start from the end of the last life lessons and continue the journey ever forward. It may feel like we're trapped in a nightmare of life after life, and it doesn't matter if you are glass half empty, glass half full, or see the glass as a way to quench a thirst and drink the water. We come here to truly feel and understand what it's like to feel love. And you may not believe this, but we all enjoy every life. And once we are out of the body, we understand every little nuance. Sometimes, it's the little things we do here that matter to the growth of a soul. Within each journey, you will find a way to understand love, and it doesn't matter what we do repeatedly or how many times we try. We eventually get there.

If that love is found with a belief in God, that's great. It can also be found in so many other places. Some of you will say God is in all these places and around us. I have thought about that God thing. He wants you to be happy, and if that love is with someone, a pet, in the mountains, in nature, or the sea, it doesn't matter. You are here to find that love because it will teach you more about yourself than anything else. I have found love in three cats, a dog, two kids, and six grandkids, and I also have a wife. (Pay attention to the order I wrote that!)

For those who think anything you do right or wrong in life is a waste, think again, because it's not. Every little thing that happens shows us something incredible about the vastness of the soul's thirst to understand and enhance its energy. It's not that bad because, at the end of each life, it's not pain. We're learning. We're learning about love in everything we do. We're not stuck. We just feel that way because love hurts.

Over the past few years, I became a part-time Spiritualist, Buddhist, and Christian. (I'm just playing the odds. I must be close to getting something right and getting in over there!) Within my work, I have listened to many good books about meditation, forgiveness, and mindfulness, and I have begun to find a way forward with some things.

I have held onto too much pain from people passing into the Spirit World, my mother being the worst. But it's as a medium that I began to see the amount of pain that other people were in, either because of their guilt of not being there with someone, not being able to see them before they passed, or not being able to help their loved ones.

I could fill this page with excuses we have for hurting ourselves with guilt and could genuinely add a million more. It's horrendous the things we can do to inflict pain and keep from moving forward with our own lives. However, the reality is this: They lived their life, and you did what you could. It doesn't matter whether they are in the light or with God. They are at peace. I cannot stress this enough. They are at peace and happy. They do not want you to stop, they do not want you to give up on life, and you haven't screwed it up. They are now in a place to understand every side of everything. Please know that they truly understand what love is. Love has no bounds, and being on the other side will not stop them from getting that love from you.

Here is an important question: "Why should you continue to hang onto something that's stopping you from living a productive life?" The answer is you shouldn't. They tell you daily that it is time for you to shine. It is time for you to be you. Trust me, they have an interest in your living. You have come here to be you, live your life, and succeed in whatever you want to do.

Ask yourself why you are hurting and suffering when they aren't. They are in a better place. Let it go bit by bit. Breathe and shine. Forgive *you*. That's my new mantra. We can only work on ourselves. So, try and release everything to let or help your love be free!

Try to accept them as Spirits fulfilling a new mission and try to understand that they are there to help you. We need to work on accepting ourselves with love. Yeah, I know it's a little easier to say than do! This is something that's stopping you from living a productive life for you. So, "forgive you."

Understand that you are love at the very core of your being. It will always be down to you. It's a choice we make daily. Do you live in pain or truth? Let's take you through something I used to think about and have said as I've grown to understand things better. My mother was always around, and I couldn't accept her leaving me. I've also seen it with people who couldn't come to terms with themselves after they had suffered because someone died. I had to find a way to move away from my pain, but I couldn't. The more I saw or felt her as Spirit, the worse it got for me. The reality was that I wasn't prepared to forgive her for leaving me here. In the end, I came up with Kit's way. You will like this!

My mantra became, "Screw her. I'm alive, and I'm going to prove to everyone she was wrong." She left me in such a way that it stopped my life until this day. However, I began to believe that this was my life, so screw her! Screw her! Screw her! Screw her! (I have a way with words, don't you think?) But then, as I grew as a person, I started to realise that I had the courage to live. I was making inroads into *living!* Hmmm, but the reality was that it wasn't peaceful. I was still in pain and taking it out on everyone else.

I had pain and no compassion for myself. The other problem was that she kept coming to see me in dreams or when I had another reading. Oh, joy! It took a long time, including a lot of alcohol and antidepressants, to realise I was still in a massive amount of pain and running away from everyone and everything in my life. That was never going to work! As my work as a medium started to impact my life, I realised that this problem may have something to do with my approach to *me*. (Did I tell you I was a fast learner?)

God our Father, Mother? It's the same look at life. They (God) sent us to learn these things, like a parent who sends us out to school. But what do we learn from all this destruction or pain we inflict on each other in the name of religion, love, war, or hate? You pick up a newspaper or watch the television news and someone is always being hurt or killed. The world has billions of people in it, and my question is, why does love have so many lessons attached to it?

The worst is that people say, "God loves you," and "He is our Father" (or Mother, depending on how you look at it). So, God, our Father and Mother, is hurting us with love? So many people say, "You, Kit, have picked these lessons." They are tailored and made for Kit, by Kit! Then why do we keep hurting ourselves if we were all choosing these lessons? Okay, this sounds like a rant…

Yes, I know it is a lot easier when we are in a place called love to achieve these things. But we come here to understand everything in a body, and it's different. Here, we cling to pain. We have ideas that others or ourselves are to blame. We have ideas that others have a right to treat us how they did/do. We walk around with pain, guilt, and hate because we live with other people's version of who we are. It's not the truth, but we get brainwashed into believing it over time.

While doing readings and working with my guides, I have discovered that just because someone is now a Spirit doesn't mean that they can walk away from the pain they have caused even after someone dies. We still have an obligation to each other to help balance out the pain and grow from it. The question is: Do we need Spirit to heal our hearts here? No, you don't, but with their help, we can move to a better place. Maybe we can learn to live a fulfilled life and love ourselves. We're here to achieve a few things, and understanding love is one of them. It's a beginning, even if that means opening our hearts to a pet.

Love is the biggest lesson in the universe. I don't need to tell any of you how hard it is to find love. If you are brave enough, you will have tried. But to find even a tiny spark of it inside, now that's the lesson. Some of us will not discover that bit for quite a few lives, but we all surrender to it. Going through everything I have experienced and coming out at the other end, discovering what I am here to do is nothing short of a miracle. But I did it. I was so lucky to be cursed/blessed/given this thing, and again, I am writing this today in a good mood! I feel that I chose to do this. Tomorrow will be another day, and if someone pisses me off, then it will be the opposite! I will hate everything I do! LOL!

I have come out the other end a little wiser and maybe more cynical, but I have come out the other side. It's with a better belief in myself, and even though my confusion or search for peace continues to this day, I keep going. But in truth, for me, it's been an up-and-down battle most days to understand the process of life and all its BS at the tender age of sixty-five I don't understand everything in the grand scheme of things! I guess I am not meant to know everything. I'm just thankful for what I know and have learned so far.

It's been exciting and confusing, but I have begun to work out some things for myself while doing this. As I have repeated time and time while working as a medium, teaching, and in this book, these are *my answers*, not anyone else's. I can tell you that not every working medium will agree, but I'm not bothered; it's what I have come to understand.

I'll leave you with this: remember that life is not a race, and it's certainly not a game. When we reach the end as a soul here, not one life before, life/love will have fulfilled itself.

"We ourselves feel that what we are doing is just a drop in the ocean. But the ocean would be less because of that missing drop."

—MOTHER TERESA

My take is that if you start to love yourself first, just think of the possibilities that await you. Love in a body and knowing love in every aspect that this place can hurl at us are the lessons in life's karma.

PART III:

HOW IT HAPPENS
FOR EVERY SOUL

I HAVE HAD so many questions about life, death, and Spirit. Having read loads of books over the years and talking with my guides, I came to an understanding that the process is:

- Soul
- Life
- Body
- Personality/Ego
- Death
- Spirit
- Soul

... and this is how it all happens for every one of us.

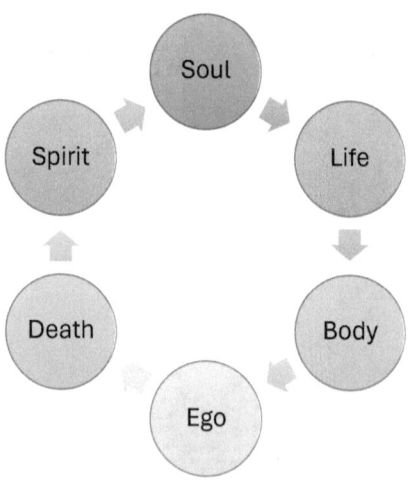

We have a body. Inside of that, we have a soul. According to Rob, the soul sits two inches below the navel. If you follow the Taoists, they say happiness starts at the belly, so he could have been right. There are other ways to look at where the soul sits. According to René Descartes, a French philosopher and scientist, it sits in the lungs, heart, pineal gland, and brain.

Then, created by the body and soul, we have a personality. It's as simple as that! I can hear you all thinking, "Okay, Mr. Clever, I get all that but explain it all!"

CHAPTER 5:

SOUL

EVERYTHING HAS A SOUL. Humans, animals, and some say even plants and trees contain one. Its energy is a spark of truth or light. The soul is so vast that it's connected to everything when not in the body; it's 100% pure consciousness out of the body. The pureness of love allows us to be one with God or Love and light in every aspect. The reality is beyond our comprehension while we are in the body, but let me try to explain it like this: When we are out of the body, we are 100% soul. However, in the body, we use, say 10-50 percent to come here and live. The rest stays there, and we know that as the *higher self,* this part of us supports our life in the body.

Our Higher Self is that part of us that remains connected to the Divine. It's the God-self within each of us... Your Higher Self is that gut feeling you get when you feel you should or shouldn't do something. It's your intuition... Your Higher Self is the space between your words, the stillness that rests within you... It's the feeling of peace you get when you stand in something beautiful... It's you beyond your ego, your insecurities, and your fears. And it's always there to guide you. It is you.

—DIANE HATZ, "Higher Self—Do You Have One?"[vii]

According to Michael Newton's books *Journey of Souls* and *Destiny of Souls*, the soul can split its energy into two and sometimes even into three incarnations simultaneously. It's interesting when you look at this theory. My question is, can we meet these other parts of ourselves while we are all here? I have been told by my guides that this is true, but you will never get to meet each other as the soul is going through a massive growth period, and each incarnation is learning so much in different areas that the soul has chosen to learn.

Now, I could go on here, but I can't explain it anymore; I honestly can't. I have become a past life regression therapist to investigate this subject. If we were full-on 100 percent of our soul when here in the body, we would be like Jesus, Buddha, or any other master who has come to make a specific change to the world and the way we live. But as I said, most of us will bring in between 10 and 50 percent, depending on the work the soul has chosen to pursue, and then when we return, we become 100 percent pure consciousness again.

Once the soul returns to the Spirit World, it will want to continue on again but spend time looking at lessons learned, and lessons and choices missed or made. Then, putting all that together, it will look at lessons to pursue in future lives.

The soul contains that piece of God we are trying to locate within us. It includes an answer to the one question we all ask: "What is life all about?" Through many lifetimes we try to remember, when all we have to do is look inside to fulfil a soul's truth. The purpose is to find our way back to God (love). The soul is the self that coexists within the body and acts through it, guiding and moving through life in tandem and, at times, driving the body forward to get the most out of each incarnation when the personality allows.

I think it's easier to say this: When you learn something here, you remember and carry it around in your memory. If it's good or bad, we learn accordingly. The soul is no different. It stores all the lives lived in its memory bank or energy field.

As Colin Bates, one of the best mediums and teachers in the world, says, we keep everything in the house of the soul. Each time we go back (die), the soul takes all the lessons learned in that life with that personality/body and stores it within its energy. It keeps every bit of information in order for it to grow and understand what it is to be in the body.

In this respect, the soul is just like our brain. It can recall anything from most of this life at any moment and sometimes just to annoy us. But the difference between the soul and the brain is that the soul can recall any lesson from any lifetime.

It will use all of this information gathered and learned when it is ready to look at another life, different from the last or past ones. It sits down with our main guide to make choices again, to come back here and become part of a new body and life, creating a new personality. It may be a different life within a different body. But it is created like this so you can change past behaviours and try new things to bring about change for all of your connections (souls) that have travelled with you time after time.

For example, for those of you like me, being in love is a minefield. We can come back time after time just to learn one little thing, so try to be kind to yourself. You may feel like life is stacked against you, but it's not. It's just bloody hard some days!

One important aspect to remember is that before we came into this life, we made these decisions with our souls, family, and friends. Again, we made those decisions as *souls*, not personalities, to help one another through love and heartache. This way, each soul gains the most from every experience, fostering growth for everyone involved.

I think the hardest thing to understand is that we come into each life blank. Our souls have been reset, and we have forgotten all our past lives to pay our debts to each other (karma). We go through everything from birth to death to grow.

From my understanding, we go through pain, pain, and more pain over and over again every time we incarnate. We also experience love of every kind, like the saying: "No pain, no gain." I know that's a flippant way to look at it, but we learn the most from every struggle. The lessons are to open us to love and to discover the truth that love is all that will ever matter. It's the universal truth. It's just that it may not feel like it all the time.

Take a look at the world. It's a beautiful place. There is so much to learn here, so much to appreciate. Go out and take a look.

CHAPTER 6:

LIFE

LIFE. WHAT IS it about? It can take many incarnations here to wake up and remember who we are, but we all get there in the end. With the help of our guides, helpers, or angels, we get the right help along the way. I can only say I come here, I go through a lot of stuff, good and bad, plus some excruciating things from time to time. Of course, I will have some excellent times because it's life, and it's designed that way by us to get the most from each time we come here.

"We're in school, so take the curriculum."

—RAM DASS, *Becoming Nobody*

We set these lessons with our guide to achieve the most in our limited time. It doesn't matter how long we are here; it could be seconds or years. We learn in the time allocated, and so does everyone connected to our lives. We create each lesson with others so they can share in our joys, losses, and achievements. In return, they get their lessons learned, too.

It's all for us to become guides, helpers, inspires, creators (not in the God sense!), or to further life here, and on the other side. There is no limit to what we can do on the other side. We will eventually become whole, part of the energy or universe, and *return to God. That's everyone's ultimate goal,* but there are so many levels of truth above that goal. At the moment, you are dealing with it there and here.

Life is mainly about learning and trying to be and do the best with what we choose each time we're here. The problem with some of us, as a species, is that we make everything so hard. We like the challenge. We want to fight, especially with ourselves or each other. We're supposed to love, but when we find it hard to feel something within, and that should always be a priority, to show that love and kindness to ourselves. Not us, though We just create pain.

We have been given one of the greatest gifts in the universe, *free will.* What do we do with it? We fight, destroy, hate, war, and be damn belligerent to be right! But that is why we are here. It takes all that to be human! In the end, we eventually become less addicted to the disorder and pain. We let life flow, and we become an integral part of each other's journey. The problem is that it takes so long and so many voyages in a body here to learn such lessons. But we do get there.

You eventually discover that life is fun and hard, but worth it. Remember this because each time we are here, we are constantly surrounded by people on their journeys. You can't avoid that. Everyone around us is growing the same way we are. It's just that they are growing with different lessons for themselves and us.

If only we could remember some of this stuff before we come here, it would be great. But we can't. We have to start with a blank page. So, the universe begins to test us differently. If we think it should be easier for us because we've attained some growth as a soul, then we're wrong.

Every lesson has energy attached to it, created in that moment for everybody in that situation. Life brings you a point of growth and it's up to you to accept it or stay in the same place. Whether you're at the top of the ladder or the bottom, life is about how we travel along this road and treat each other.

Look at something as simple as this: we are often on one side of an argument and then another, and we will agree with certain people. That's life, right? We become a part of one group more than the other in that aspect of life—for example, politics, sport, the environment, or we like a TV show others don't. We can disagree about absolutely anything. Nothing wrong with that. It is something that is part of the design. It is life. Take that thought even further. We are made up of males and females, of blacks, whites, and Asians, to name just a few. This might help you understand that you take up a particular position or opposition in anything that comes your way in your life. To fully understand everything, you choose the opposite next time you come here.

If you go back to the list (male, female, black, white, Asian), you have to understand everything life offers. It may take you one thousand lifetimes, but you get there. You learn who you are here and take that to the other side, file it away, and start again a little wiser. Maybe a little kinder too, but always wiser.

CHAPTER 7:

BODY

OUR BODIES ARE created for the soul to achieve its goals and balance the universe from each soul's perspective. With the help of our guides and the understanding of the work we want to do here, we sit down and discuss everything, then pick one. The relationship is symbiotic. Together, the body, soul, and personality/ego become one for growth on this plane. Interestingly, no matter what we think about our body (we can love or hate it) it is always the right one because we chose it with its lumps and bumps to work out things through it!

Without the soul, the body is an empty vessel and cannot survive. It is the vehicle we move around. It's a very technical achievement that has taken millions of years of evolution to perfect. It's a shame that we treat it with such disdain, but even that is a part of the soul's growth. We must learn to love every part of each body.

CHAPTER 8:

PERSONALITY/EGO

THE PERSONALITY, OR EGO. We have a body to come here. The soul comes in to take a journey and to live a life. The soul and the body, along with each lesson and each choice we make, create a personality or ego. I think *personality* sounds better because it is the personality I'm talking to as a medium. Each time we come here, that personality differs from the last one. The lessons continue from where the previous life lessons ended but with a few more added. Some are to check to see if you can do things differently and some are for progression. Because we create each life to facilitate the growth of the soul, it doesn't matter how many we have.

Everybody's personality is a combination of characteristics, some good and some bad, that form a person's distinctive disposition, character, or personality. These qualities make us unique as human beings to our loved ones here. This is the bit we have been developing since we were babies here on the Earth plane.

Many words describe this as humans, which can be a highly complex part of us. Here are a few to help you understand what I am talking about: character, charisma, magnetism, disposition, temperament, presence, and charm. Then we have kind, pleasant, lovely, mean, nasty, and horrible, just to name a few. The list could go on, but all the parts described make up an individual like you and me.

As a medium, I get asked every time I teach to explain this one. I think I may have a decent enough answer thanks to my teacher, Rob Brown, and Nat's teacher, Colin Bates. (Thank you to you both.) When you visit a medium for a reading, you want to talk to the Spirit World. For example, you have a lady come to you for a reading, and she wants to contact her mum. So, you do your medium stuff. Now, at this point, you are talking through your personality, and it is her personality you will be reaching out to because whoever your sitter (person having a reading) wants to talk to would have known them as a mum! However, in reality, you are using your soul as a medium to connect to the soul of the sitter's mum. It is that soul allowing the personality from that life to come forward for the reading to prove who they were in life. So, your sitter knows that this is her mum, and she is okay.

Let's see if I can try that again and explain more. Present are the:

1. Medium.
2. Sitter, or person having a reading.
3. Soul and personality/ego of loved one.

Let me clarify. As a medium, I may give a reading that appears to be a personality-to-personality exchange, but I believe it's genuinely a soul-to-soul connection. When a soul or Spirit comes through in a reading, their goal is often to show their loved one (the sitter) that they have survived death and are at peace on the other side. They do this by providing evidence through the medium, using their personality in their last life to communicate with the sitter. Once they've established that connection, the next part of the reading is delivering the message. This message is intended to support the sitter's personality as they navigate challenges or phases in life and grief. If you're trained as a coach or therapist, this is where all your skills come into play to help guide the sitter.

Now, as to why they don't need to address the soul of the sitter: even though I'm talking to a Spirit, I am talking to the soul. If I were to describe the soul to the person sitting there in front of me, they would have no idea who I was talking about. So, the soul or Spirit that allows me to talk to the personality is connected. The interesting thing here is that personality will be sending a message from the soul because your soul needs to know that it's time to move, it's time to do things. This is complicated to explain but it's called *soul-to-soul reading*.

The soul inherently knows its path. With its free will, the personality creates resistance, questioning, doubting, or stalling progress due to the fears it holds within its energy. That doesn't mean the soul or higher self isn't aligned with the message. It recognises and supports it, having been working toward these same goals. The sitter's guides, too, are glad to assist in moving things forward. Everyone's soul knows what it's supposed to be doing, the lessons it will be facing, and the truth of what it is here to do. Still, the personality/ego always wants to be involved because, as most of us know, the ego knows everything. But as you know, it doesn't know anything.

My personal experiences with my soul have pushed me to make major changes throughout my life. But my fears of failure, of looking stupid, and of totally doubting my abilities have held me back, and that's been down to my personality.

In a reading, everyone wants to know that we are okay on the other side. If they are open to visiting someone like me, a medium, they can get confirmation. If not, there are many different ways for them to know.

I speak to my mum, family, and friends in my dreams and my head. So, don't doubt yourself. You are always talking to your loved ones. I've had a bit of training to access it deeper but trust yourself and believe they are always with you.

I constantly hear people saying things like:

"My God, I hope this is my last life!"

"I'm never coming back."

"This place is horrible."

"I hate it here."

"I hate people."

"I don't want to keep doing this."

"This is too hard!"

This is the personality talking because it holds all that fear and wants it all to end. The good thing is that it's the soul making the journey, not the personality. I think that one massive thing happens when we leave here: The soul will get up to the other side and know that this life just lived was *amazing*. It will know it has gained purpose and want to try something else.

"Like Freud and Erikson, Jung regarded the psyche as made up of a number of separate but interacting systems. The three main ones were the ego, the personal unconscious, and the collective unconscious."

—SAUL MCLEOD PhD, *Carl Jung's Theory of Personality: Archetypes & Collective Unconscious*

Many have tried to understand the brain and the ego. The three mentioned above—Freud, Erikson, and Jung—believed in the ego, the personal unconscious, and the collective unconscious. Suppose you look at how a person navigates the world with the ego (personality, personal unconscious), soul, and collective unconscious (Spirit). In that case, they have a point and are correct.

CHAPTER 9:

DEATH

"The purpose of death is to die into love."

—RAM DASS, *Becoming Nobody*

DEATH IS AN interesting conversation starter in everyday life for me. It's something I can't avoid as a medium or as a grief coach. And no, death doesn't happen. Well, it does, but it's just the body that dies, nothing else. The body has a life span, and we can extend it to a point by looking after it. We can also lessen the pain, illness, or suffering, but at the end of the day, we all die. At the same time, the truth is nothing ever dies. It changes back into Spirit, then love, and moves on to the next realm, heaven, dimension, universe, or afterlife, and becomes an entire soul again. As simple as that.

Death is such an emotionally painful thing to us all, and that includes the person dying. They know they are about to leave us, and nobody wants to leave anybody behind. Nobody wants to die. It's just part of the process. It's as horrible as that, as we lose our loved ones and now have to face each day without that love. But in the grand scheme of things, it is such a glorious event in the life of a soul. It's the end to just one part of our truth, of who we truly are at the core of our being.

When each life ends, the soul returns to discuss what it has learned. Just so you know, it is NOT JUDGED BY ANYONE, NOT EVEN BY OURSELVES! It is learning what it did, how it moved through its journey, and how it affected everyone connected to it. All this is about is to see if we could have done anything different. It is crucial to know that we are never judged by anyone else. Everything is examined and looked at by ourselves. We look at the karma we have created and cleared, then start planning our next incarnation to balance the universe with all the souls involved in our journeys, and on to the next incarnation we go. Our guide looks at everything because they know what we want to learn. You could look at it like it's one big therapy session.

I'll try to give this a bit of perspective, and I said *try*. Lessons don't stop at the end of life. As humans, we all end life with a lot of unresolved, and for want of a better word, *stuff*. At the top of the list are things we regret, words we wish we hadn't said, and words we could have or should have said, like, "I'm sorry," or "I love you!"

There are things in our hearts that we should have done and, certainly, things we shouldn't have done, but for one reason or another, we didn't have the courage. We go to the other side to heal, rest, and regroup with our loved ones and guides; to eventually plan our next adventure back here! In the meantime, in the Spirit World, we all need to heal all of the above.

It's been said that death is a big adventure, and I suppose it's true. Deep within each of us, it's just something we already know about on a soul level. We just have fears because we don't want to face the reality that we are mortals here and immortal there.

Nothing terrible is going to happen. That is just a lot of what people have been told through religion. They say that the big man in the sky who created us in his image is angry with us because we failed him. Let me tell you that he is proud of every one of us for taking this journey. He is happy that we want to expand our knowledge about ourselves daily and to help the universe expand.

Don't be afraid to live.

The one problem some of us have is that we fear living an incredible life and forego astonishing growth in our journeys. But there is nothing to fear about death. It's just a door back to our true essence, then recharges, regroups, and onto a different journey. In all honesty, it's a return to sanity and from the corruption in this place. We have all come here to have an adventure. We have come to take part in finding an answer to a question. The question is not, "What is life?" but "Who am I?" Part of the answer is that you are love, and deep at the centre, you are truth. You're here to learn all of this and so much more. You are here to learn about love, and *it starts with loving you first*. Please, please don't live in fear. Move forward and live with truth, knowing you are fantastic no matter what anybody else thinks, says, or does. Your soul is at the centre of who you are and will thank you, and so will your God.

CHAPTER 10:

SPIRIT

WHEN OUR PHYSICAL existence comes to an end for this life (death), we go back to, well, take your pick: the Spirit World, heaven, arcadia, Canaan, Elysium, Shangri-La, Utopia, Zion, the afterworld, Azure Dreamland, our eternal home, eternal rest, eternity, fairyland, the great unknown, hunting ground, hereafter, God's kingdom, Jannah, the next world, nirvana, paradise, the pearly gates, the promised land, upstairs, and wonderland, to name just a few. For me, we return to the Spirit World.

Spirit is the form we return to and the human word and understanding for it. Over there, we probably call it something completely different! There are so many other books and articles about people having near-death experiences and leaving their bodies and seeing themselves as Spirits floating down a long corridor. Then there are so many daily reports of people seeing Spirits or ghost shows on TV, so that's what we call it: Spirit.

If we use some of these reports and books as an example, when we step out of the body, we float up and down a tunnel and arrive to be surrounded by all our loved ones and friends—knowing we've now reached the Spirit World. It is beautifully explained how things happen to us. However, if we look at it a little bit closer, now of death, we leave the body as Spirit. For most of us, we are still the personality because that is who we believe or think we are. Then, we float down the tunnel, arrive at the other end, and reunite with the rest of our soul or higher self.

As I have explained, when we come here, we only use a percentage of the soul's energy to travel out and have a life. While on each journey, the rest stays there. This again, is called your *higher self*. So, the soul becomes whole, the personality becomes part of the lessons learned and filed away into the soul's memory, and we move forward. We move on to other things and plan for the next adventure.

If you have read the previous pages, this should all now come together.

If I were to be honest, it's working as a medium that I have found the most interesting, mind-blowing, annoying, frustrating, uplifting, depressing, and glorious side to me! Working with Spirit has its significant drawbacks, and any medium or healer out there understands that we play our part, and they play theirs.

This is a joint adventure and journey. I do not work *for* Spirit, and they do not work for me. At the end of the day, you are in the body and can reject their input at any point in life! You do not need to kiss Spirits' arse because you believe they are in a better place (the Spirit World) and must be all-knowing. They are not.

There are vibrations above them, and we are all trying to reach that point. Then, when we get there, we will try to reach the next point. Please don't ask me about these other places. I only understand these two, maybe three places, and I'm not a great authority on them. I'm a student of life and love, just like you. How do I know these places exist? I don't, but if we are just trying to get to the next place, then back here, then back there, what would that be like? YES, boring!

Just think about that, then look at what we have done here. We have created a hierarchy of learning as humans here on this plane of existence. We go to school, we pass tests, and we get to a high place in life because we are trying to achieve greatness—a better life for ourselves and our families, houses, cars, holidays, or whatever we want to do in life, whatever our dreams are.

We are taught to try to get somewhere in life and be someone. It's a human thing to want more and be better at whatever our chosen field is. That's what we are taught by our parents, teachers, and friends or peers. Life becomes a competition to be the best at whatever we do. If we come here to learn about everything as souls, *this is a school.* When we are finished coming here as a student, we become something else: a guide, a teacher, the list goes on. But again, that's just another learning we encounter. Not just to progress a single planet but to move an entire universe into the truth that love is all that will ever be. We are trying to reach the fullness and what it is to be whole again.

Our universe as we know it is small compared to reality, to the wisdom and knowledge that we can tap into with our limited brains. If energy is infinite and we are limited by our thoughts, we could strive to do so much better with this thing called life. If we conquer the ego that drives us crazy at the best and worst times, I say good luck with that!

No matter who we are as humans (not everybody, but for the most part, and I am including myself in this), from time to time, we become a bit disgruntled. We can be an unhappy species. The reality is that we have a fast amount of greatness at our fingertips. We have the chance to do something incredible together or on our own, yet for some of us, here we are day in and day out, not doing anything of importance!

That's also what's so amazing about life. In every breath, every second, every moment, minute, hour, day, week, month, and year, we choose to take part or not. We choose time after time, each life we come here. Lucky for us, eventually, our soul gets bored and really wants to do something for itself and everyone involved. So, it will program it into its system as it starts each new life. If you look at the bigger picture, nothing is ever wasted here. Not one bit of energy is lost. Everything is used to harmonise the reality of life, and one day, this place we call Earth will balance life of every kind and be revered and respected.

The real thing to remember about everyone on the other side, including you and your relatives, is that we have been here many times. To put it into perspective, each guide or helper had to experience the same as you and I. Yes, they too have been through the trials and tribulations of life. They have felt loss, pain, hurt, and depression, and they made it through. So, remember, you and I can too.

When working with them, they have as much invested in this relationship as we do. They chose to be a part of your journey to learn something to help someone else. This experience is a win-win for both sides. Having worked with my team for my entire life, I can tell you that they have felt everything I have and have been just as frustrated watching me stumble around trying to find the light.

You have been a part of something every day of your life, and it would be a pretty poor world if you were not allowed to think for yourself and redefine who you are in the universe. So, let go of the BS of life and the stuff that holds you in place and soar. If nothing else, you may just find an interesting new thing about you. And even if you do fall, they will catch you. The problem is you won't find out how they caught you until it's over and you're over there, but they will be there with you.

The Spirit World is not hard to understand, but it took me a while to get my head around this as I had always been told God was looking "down on me." After repeatedly seeing little balls of light (orbs) flash all around me for most of my life, I realised I was catching energy moving faster than me. After talking to my teachers, guide, and all my helpers, I discovered it was right here with us, it was just going faster than we were. The Spirit World is not on a distant planet or in the heavens above us in the sky. It's not millions of miles from Earth. We occupy the same space as this world, it's just another realm, another vibration or dimension. The easiest way to understand it is to think of us vibrating at one level and them at another. We can't always see them because they're moving faster than us.

In the Spirit World, there is no pain, death, or hate. Love matters, nothing else. And yes, every animal goes there, why shouldn't they? I believe every insect, tree, plant, and anything here will have a place there. Everything that exists in our environment is part of a chain of existence and contributes to the planet's survival. Ultimately, we all return to where we originally came from, and it doesn't matter which religion you celebrate life with here. We all come from the same place and go back there. No one is left behind or left out, and everyone will be given light and love, no matter what we believe in or do here.

The only ones who don't think this are atheists. They say they don't have a belief. They say nothing happens after we die. What can I say? I like it, but it's not my belief. And as my therapist, Tony from Derby used to say, in truth, *atheism is a belief* anyway, and they're still going there!

Love is the truth. Even the most hateful of us eventually feel love.

PART IV:

SPIRITUALISM

CHAPTER 11:

A BRIEF HISTORY & THE PRINCIPLES

"Spiritualism is a religion that embodies the main ideas of all religions, that there is a life after death, immortality and the existence of a God."

—With kind permission from Minister Steven Upton, Public Relations Officer, and The Spiritualist National Union

THERE ARE MANY paths to God, and Spiritualism is just another. We are not worshipping false profits or, as it says in the Bible, "You shall have no other gods before me." Spiritualism is where we go to hear other mediums speak their truth. And just so you know, not every medium has come through the church. Nat and I have. We thought it would add to the background of who we are. It is a way in which we celebrate our truth, the same as any other religion. Sometimes, we just want somewhere to be with like-minded people. We still go to regular church. I love going to the Catholic Church and just sitting there hearing the hymns.

We all need to understand where we have come from, and it would not be right if we didn't recognise the struggles mediums have gone through over the years to be accepted in today's world—well, nearly accepted! These great, illustrious people did so much for our movement and for religion, often sacrificing a great deal. It is our responsibility to understand who these pioneers were and be able to discuss their significance within our work. I may sound old now, but certain people risked their lives and reputations to prove that life indeed does carry on after the death of the body and that God is a part of our lives (as is also postulated by other religions around the world).

Mediums from the early days went through immense struggles. In one particular case, Helen Duncan was persecuted and prosecuted under the Witchcraft Act of 1735. She was convicted of conspiracy to "pretend to conjure up the dead."

Emma Hardinge Britten was born Emma Floyd in London, England, in 1823. Through trance and mediumship, she laid down the original Principles of Spiritualism. They came through with the help of a Spirit, Mr. Robert Owen, who was deceased, and those first Principles were passed through mediumship communication. The same Robert

Owen championed Mrs. Marie Hayden in his publication, *The Rational Quarterly Review.*

These Principles all contribute to a belief system that mediums who attend services and are followers of Spiritualism are proud to be a part of. The real point to them is that God has given all of us on this planet a life, and it is up to us to decide how we live it. These Principles are a guiding example to this world and the next.

These are the original Principles:

The Fatherhood of God

The Brotherhood of Man

The Immortality of the Soul and its Personal Characteristics

The Proven Facts of Communion Between Departed Human Spirits and Mortals

Personal Responsibility with Compensation and Retribution Hereafter for All the Good and Evil Deeds Done Here

A Path of Eternal Progress Open to Every Human Soul that Wills to Tread it by the Path of Eternal Good

Andrew Jackson Davis formed the basis for modern Spiritualism's philosophy primarily through his 1847 book, *The Principles of Nature: Her Divine Revelations*, and a *Voice to Mankind*, dictated in a trance, which outlined his "Harmonial Philosophy," connecting science, religion, and spirit, and established concepts like the "Summerland," becoming the intellectual foundation for the growing movement that gained mainstream attention with the Fox sisters in 1848.

"Summerland is a Spiritualist term referring to a paradisal after-death state. It first appeared in 1845 in the published automatic writings of the youthful Andrew Jackson Davis, the "Poughkeepsie Seer." One of several concentric spherical planes surrounding the earth, the Summerland is the habitation of spirits of good will. Descriptions by mediumistic communicators present the deceased as living a harmonious, quasi-physical life amid supernally beautiful houses, lecture halls, music, gardens, meadows, trees, lakes, streams, and animals. Like other spheres, the Summerland is a product of the minds of its inhabitants. A basic principle of Spiritualism is that "like attracts like"; thus, deceased persons who are attuned to beauty, love, and learning are drawn together, and singly or in concert they create these delights, which appear to be altogether concrete. A spirit residing in this sphere may communicate with the living for their benefit; likewise, living persons while out-of-body may upon occasion visit the Summerland.[viii]"

The Fox sisters—Margaretta, age 15, and Catherine (Kate), age 12—lived with their parents in Hydesville (near Rochester), in upstate New York, USA. They moved into their house in December 1847 and were immediately troubled by knocking on the table and objects moving around it. After initially being scared, the two children quickly discovered that if they spoke out loud, they could get a response, either by rapping on a table or door. It was in late March 1848 that the Fox sisters finally established two-way communication with a man who was said to have been haunting the house for several years before their family moved in. It did not take long for the news to spread about the incidents.

In the following years, many societies were formed in the USA to research and discuss this so-called *mediumship* or *rapping*. Other groups were formed to seek out psychic, spiritual, and religious growth. Not long after that, we started to openly get the first Spiritualist Churches in the USA and UK.

American medium Maria B. Hayden brought Spiritualism and her unique mediumship (healing, clairvoyance, spirit communication) to England in the autumn (October) of 1852, arriving in London and holding séances that attracted elites, clergy, and scientists, significantly influencing the British Spiritualist movement despite initial skepticism. Mrs. Hayden, having brought her version of mediumship to England, used it in public demonstrations. However, the newspapers and some prominent Christian church members ridiculed her. She still had her supporters, one being Robert Owen, a social reformer at eighty-three, who declared his new faith in his publication, *The Rational Quarterly Review*, after witnessing Mrs Hayden's mediumship. He later wrote about this in a pamphlet titled, "The Future of the Human Race, or Great Glorious and Future Revolution to be Effected through the Agency of Departed Spirits of Good and Superior Men and Women."

In 1853, David Richmond brought Spiritualism to the attention of the people of Keighley in West Yorkshire. With the assistance of David Weatherhead, Richmond delivered three lectures on the subject at the Working Men's Hall in June 1853. Weatherhead took steps, forming a society called The Spiritual Brotherhood, later becoming The Heber Street Spiritualist Society as it remains today.

Alfred Kitson (1855 – 1934) was the first Secretary of the Spiritualists' Lyceum Union and known as 'Dad Kitson,' the Father of the British Lyceum Movement in the UK. Born in Gawthorpe, Yorkshire, Alfred was brought up as a strict Methodist. His father investigated mediums and Spiritualism, looking to find evidence of fraud. Instead, he developed as a medium! (Hmmm, Spirit moves in funny ways. What a sense of humour they have.) Alfred devoted his efforts to working with children and the Lyceum. He wrote several books on the subject and copies are held in the Lyceum Library at AFC Stanstead. His system for teaching was initially founded in the United States by Andrew Jackson Davis around 1863.

Marcellus Seth Ayer founded the First Temple in the USA on June 28th, 1883. It was an independent Christian Spiritualist Church. The original church was built on the corner of Exeter and Newbury Streets in the Back Bay area in Boston, Massachusetts. It has now been relocated to Brookline, and along with the move went the cornerstone laid on April 9th, 1884.

Today, mediumship continues to expand with the help of the Spiritualists' National Union (SNU), Christian Spiritualists, Corinthians, and spiritual people, opening centres in community halls, working men's clubs, and even pubs. This is happening all over the world, allowing mediumship to develop well.

Eventually, the Principles were changed and have remained the same since. When doing Divine Services, most mediums will base their philosophy on the revised Principles below:

The Fatherhood of God

The Brotherhood of Man

The Communion of Spirits and the Ministry of Angels

The Continuous Existence of the Human Soul

Personal Responsibility

Compensation and Retribution Hereafter for all the Good and Evil Deeds Done on Earth

Eternal Progress Open to every Human Soul

Metaphysical churches in the USA have their variations, but for most churches we have served, the congregation reads the Principles before each Sunday service. We have not added them here due to copyright law, but you can visit any Spiritualist Church in the USA and get a warm welcome.

The Principles of Spiritualism do not offer an alternative to the Ten Commandments. They have been handed down from Spirit and passed through one of our great pioneers, offering a different way to look at life. When looking at the difference, I suppose it comes down to being told what to do and having the free will to live how you want. Like Buddhism, Christianity, Catholicism, Judaism, Islam, and Sikhism, Spiritualism has a significant history and a set of principles to our faith, no different from any other religion.

I prefer Ricky Gervais' film *The Invention of Lying* and from that film, the "Ten Rules," along with "The Man in the Sky," but that's me. I truly believe that God has a sense of humour and gets it big time. Otherwise, he would not have created us. Thank you, Ricky, bloody hilarious.

IF YOU WANT to look at the history more deeply, look at Harry Houdini and Sir Arthur Conan Doyle. I would have liked to add so much more about the past mediums, but how long is a piece of string? Where do you start and finish? It would make for great reading, an anthology of the illustrious greats of mediumship. Maybe somebody else should write it.

Chapter 12:

How It All Works

PSYCHICS RECEIVE OR draw their information from the living vibrations of energy around them at Earthly levels. *Mediums* adjust their level of consciousness, paying acute attention mentally to higher, faster energy vibrations. By doing so, they receive information outside the customary normal communication levels used by mankind. It is like turning your head into a receiver. The *medium* changes mental consciousness frequency so that, when attuned, communication received from the Spirit World can be passed on verbally. The medium then becomes a receiving and transmitting station, with no license fees to pay! But—as with a TV set—the instrument (the medium) has to learn how to control the frequency in use to maintain control of any possible atmospheric interference.

People have debated for a long time if one can be both a *psychic* and a *medium*. Well, there is a saying we were all taught:

All mediums are psychics,
but not all psychics are mediums.

I believe we're all receiving information from the Spirit World most of the time. Having had readings from both mediums and psychics and being able to do both, I believe if you are willing to open your mind, then anything is possible. It is all about sitting, meditating, and retraining to receive from a source outside oneself. You can understand the difference between *medium* and *psychic* by training and doing exercises. Some people are very gifted and get it from the start. Some, like me, have to understand how it all works.

A LEADING SPIRIT *guide* is assigned to us at the start of our birth or creation in the Spirit World. It helps us make plans/decisions before we come into every life and genuinely understand who we are and where we are going. We sit together to discuss and determine what we want to achieve next in the body. This includes pain and sorrow, laughter, more pain and sorrow—yes, I'm still cynical—and choices we must make to progress as a soul.

A guide is not there to tell you what to do in your life. They generally step back as this is your incarnation and you're learning journey. However, there are times when they step in to help. At those times in my life, I did not understand or know, but later, I understood why they had intervened or shown me a different direction. (And just so you know, it was a very subtle shove.)

I have been told over the years that I have as many as ten guides working with me at any one time. Then, I was told that I have five! I believe I have one main guide and many other Spirits, helpers, and teachers who come in as I do different things. These helpers come close to me with my work as a teacher and coach, and just as a human being. It doesn't matter who you are or what you do in life. We are all blessed with guides, and they come in from the other side to offer help to get us through this life and every life we choose to live.

John is my Spirit guide, and we work as a team to help people through mediumship and coaching. He comes through as a monk dressed in dark robes. It is a description that many mediums and students alike have given me. It will often go like this: A dark figure stands behind me. He looks dark and scary. I can't see his face, but I can tell you that he is all love and my true friend in this world. I believe we shared a life as Gregorian monks. He chose this guise because he enjoyed that past life. We have known each other all this life, and as I believe in my truth, he has been my guide in every incarnation I have ever had.

I also believe that my granddad and grandma are working with me. They come around as helpers when I need them, such as when things go wrong or go great. My grandma is there, especially if I need to be told off—so most days she appears! They are a part of me as much as I am a part of them, and yes, they can be intelligent asses too.

Others who come around to help me when I teach are my brother Nicky, my friend Cyril, and from time to time, a little boy called Logan. I also have other higher beings helping me with a presentation.

I believe that John brings in these higher beings of light to teach me the philosophy of healing and answer questions when I am working. He is at the heart of all my work. He is my driving force and someone I am quite positive will love, scream, shout, or moan at me as I continue to make a mess of life. As I'm writing this, he reminds me that I swear a lot at him, and as I continue to write, he tells me he will never judge me but is there to love me unconditionally. Your guide will always do the same for you. They will love and support you no matter what you do in this incarnation.

I always turn to John for help, guidance, love, and support. When I hit my lowest, I know he will be there for me. Yes, there are people out there who look at the way I am with my guide and say I should have more respect. But for those, I say that this is how I am and how he knows me. It has not been an easy journey for me or those around me on this side or over there, but I'm doing the best with what I have. They, in turn, are doing the same and have gotten the worst of this deal! Trust me, I know exactly what I'm like!

In the USA and never anywhere else, I am always asked how I contact my guide and how I know his name. I'm no different from many mediums out there; I never felt the need to get his name. In several readings and workshops, I was told what he looked like and, eventually, his name. For me, that was enough. In truth, I wasn't that interested because we worked together as one, before and after I knew.

How do you contact *your* guide? If you go into the silence and breathe, you will hear a voice hovering above your mind. It will have gentle vibrations all its own. It may take you a long time to do this—in some cases, it will not be instant—but eventually, as you grow, so will this vibration. You can test it at first with little questions, but as you become more proficient at being a medium, the voice will become a dependable friend in a mishmash of noise.

PEOPLE ALWAYS ASK me who my *angel* is, and if he is what a medium calls a *guide*. This is understandable since they are both sent or given to us as humans to help while in an incarnation (living). They support us through tough times, helping us stand tall and achieve what we want. However, there is a difference: A *guide* is with us before we come into this life, while an *angel* is a messenger who comes in times of need.

One of my favourite films depicting this is *It's a Wonderful Life*. In it, the angel Clarence saves Jimmy Stewart's character, George Bailey, from committing suicide by jumping off a bridge. There are stories from all over the world of angels being there to help people or catch them in times of trouble. So, guides are around us most of the time. Angels appear from time to time, in forms that we will not get until after, or never. They can even have a human appearance, like in another Christmas film, *The Bishop's Wife*.

Angels are here now, guiding this planet and its leaders to take the Earth to another level of consciousness. We have been struggling for a long time now and need to make some changes. It is my understanding from all the work we are involved in that they are doing this through all of us, helping us find a new consciousness and ways to help each other and save the Earth.

SO, HOW DOES Spirit communication work? Look at how radio waves broadcast music through the air, often over continents and even into space. As a medium, we can have conversations with the Spirit World because of the way the frequency of physical and non-physical blend together. Communication with Spirit is done through the blending of the two energies, with the use of emotional and mental energy. For this to work in the medium (physical), we must increase our vibration and Spirit (non-physical) will lower theirs. The two will blend at this point, allowing us to work in tandem and exchange information. It takes time to build up a relationship and a constant stream of information.

"Focus of the mind—energy follows thought; create a positive co-operative feeling towards the Spirit World. Empower your mediumship through the use of intuitive, psychic and spiritual power. Focus on the changes that take place in you. Also, remember to question the changes."

—COLIN BATES, a medium friend and great teacher

MEDITATION IS A straightforward way to get you to hear the silence inside, to look for a little voice gently talking to you. The problem when starting any meditation is the silence, mainly trying to find it! All you hear at the start is your mind trying to break in (monkey-mind). All it's doing is kicking in, trying to get you to think about anything and everything to stop you.

As writer, Buddhist, and meditation teacher Jack Kornfield says, the brain has no shame, and that's so true. I have found it easier to let it do what it wants and let the thoughts flow through. An easy thing to do is to count backward from 100. Every time a thought steps in, start counting again. Time each number with a breath in. All you're looking for is ten minutes a day of practice. Just treat yourself for some time and see who is around.

I used to teach meditation for a couple of companies, and I loved it. I had so many amazing reports that people were able to go and sit at their desks, be calmer, and face their work in a different way. Please don't take my word for it. If you can join a meditation class, get used to doing this with others, or do a guided meditation, this can be incredibly useful as time goes on. This is what you'll be looking for anyway.

Not only is meditation good for your search for that inner voice, but it can also be so good in helping you find a new and calmer you. I could list many benefits of meditation, but these are the amazing things you will discover about yourself. There are several essential benefits to releasing stress from our bodies and brain.

Doing meditation regularly leads you to a deeper level of relaxation and contemplation. If you want to be free of constant worry, pressure, and stress, meditation can give you a calm, peaceful, happy, and relaxed life. Even five to ten minutes a day helps alleviate a hell of a lot of stuff while also helping you find the inner voice of Spirit.

You'll hear a lot of talk from teachers of mediumship about how you're sitting in power. You're learning all about your inner power and strengths, moving your mind and body into a different level of thought and contemplation. Don't push yourself to go crazy and get annoyed when you can't get it right some days.

Being gentle with yourself a couple of times a week is fantastic. Even if you're just sitting there looking out the window or sitting somewhere calm and relaxing, you're still being with you, and remember being with you. You'll start to notice how close the Spirit is to you, so you're still gaining from these brief moments, as are your loved ones and guides.

Just so you know, going to church, sitting in silence, and praying is meditation. Sitting in the garden or gardening, washing pots and pans, and ironing—all these things you do enable active meditation. So, when you think you can't do it, nine times out of ten, you are already doing it in some kind of way.

ANOTHER COMMON QUESTION I am often asked is, "Can our loved ones or spouses who have passed help us find new love? The simple answer to this is yes, but the problem for some of us here is that we feel the need to move on and love again straight away. Society has sadly impressed on us that if we are not with someone, we are sad or weird. Or if we don't find somebody quickly, we will be left on the shelf to die lonely, old, and miserable!

It doesn't matter how long we were married or together. We have to understand that they have passed over. We have to deal with shit from other people alone and not as a couple. They are not holding us when the world is kicking the door down. Well, in truth, they are holding us, but you don't feel it the same because they are not in the physical realm where we get the sensation of touch; they are on another plane of existence.

To help with the loneliness, we may rush in with the first or second person who comes along and takes an interest in us. For some, it can lead to a broken heart again. We get disillusioned and find ourselves back at the start, lonely and in more pain.

Moving on and finding new love is a product of numerous things. It may depend on how far you are in your mourning or whether you are ready to begin again. Be assured that if a new relationship is something you want in life, Spirit will help.

Please remember this: Your spouse is in a better place to understand what you need first. Having lived with you, they understand you better than most. What we often forget is that we have to love and know ourselves first. We have to find love for ourselves and the peace of knowing who we are as an individual before anything else. Only then will our loved ones help.

I can promise they will be on the front row bringing in love. They know what makes you tick, and they certainly know what will work for your heart. Who better to help you find new love than the one who loved you before? Whether it's love and companionship, a new best friend, or someone to share life with again, they will assist you in finding that love.

The psychological damage that arises from the death of someone is incredible. Not only are we dealing with the death, but it can then bring up every piece of crap from our lives. Anyone dead or alive whoever did anything wrong, abused, hurt, or picked on us in any way will come crashing to the surface of our thoughts. We are in our most vulnerable place ever. Our minds fall apart, and we relive that pain over and over daily.

At this point, we must get rid of the baggage we may have carried around since we were children. Trust me, now is the time to do it. One of the main things I am advised by Spirit to tell you in a reading is to seek professional help. Find a therapist and get help. You will not get any of this stuff out of the way unless you deal with it, and you will not find the love you seek. Your priority at this moment is to learn to love and accept *you*. The time has come to put all your pain away.

On a side note, please remember that it's okay to see people for readings. However, it becomes a little bit dangerous (for everyone involved) if you are there every week and someone else is making decisions for you because you are afraid of getting it wrong!

Before you think I am just making this up, I can tell you from my experience that there was a time when I would ring someone or see someone at least once a week. I lost control and thought I was in jeopardy of making a mistake in everything I did! I became obsessed with karma and feared I would make the wrong choice.

We all need to remember that we are here, and we make choices that are not wrong. We can't go wrong. We make a decision and move forward. If it doesn't work out, we make another. We are not failures: none of us. We just make a new choice again and try a different way.

Visiting a medium or psychic reader of any kind should be considered carefully and done for the right reasons. When things go wrong, we want help to fix it quickly. Should I move house, state, or country? Will they come back? These are all good questions. As readers, we are there to help.

If your medium or psychic has trained as a coach or therapist, that's even better because they will not tell you what to do but help you find your way. However, there does come a time when we have to sit down and ask ourselves what to do next. Sitting down with someone and looking at everything once is great, but you must step forward. Trust yourself and believe in yourself. After all, it is *your* life.

Do your homework. Learn who you are and what you want. The Spirit World and your lost love will guide you back to happiness.

I AM OFTEN asked if children have psychic or mediumship experiences. The answer is yes, and it can be terrifying for them. My first experience goes back to when I was seven, after my mother passed and appeared at the bottom of my bed and scared the crap out of me. It is difficult for people to understand that children could have mediumistic or psychic gifts. We have had children in the movement of Spiritualists for over 150 years, so we should be embracing them into the fold and not shunning them and making them feel like they are mad or worse, cursed by evil Spirits and possessed by demons.

Children need to find a teacher the same as adults and get into a class with a reputable mentor. Working with children is a specialty and should always be done with parents present. Both need to understand that these gifts come with many responsibilities, problems, and a commitment. The parents need to work with their children so that all involved understand this is normal.

Just so you understand, we are all normal, whether we are adults or children. But our children need to understand that we are doing work for our souls and the universe. And our souls have chosen to do this work at this time to help each other spiritually. So, relax they are not freaks of nature. Both my children and grandchildren have amazing gifts. I have not sought to push them in any way, and my children have not pushed their children in any way to develop, either. My kids would be the first to find all the help and understanding they can to guide my grandkids in the same way I have done for them.

It's just so hard being a parent in this day and age, when we're surrounded by people constantly finger-pointing at anyone who is different, and it's getting worse. We need to encourage people to be different and our children to be magnificent in their individuality, not to be the same. We're not bloody robots. We're all here to contribute in our own way, and does it really matter what we believe in?

Adults and children also need to understand the importance of controlling their energy within this work. I am a big believer in keeping our energy "closed down" (see later in this book) until I have to work. My advice is to gain control over the way you work with Spirit because if you don't, it will drive you crazy, and I mean crazy as an adult, let alone a child!

PART V:

AURAS & CHAKRAS

CHAPTER 13:

AURAS

THE NEXT BIT is going to be answered by Rob, as you have already heard a lot about him in this book. He was and still is my best friend and teacher. However, it was with great sadness that while I was working on this book, he sadly, and I mean sadly for everyone connected to his life, passed with liver cancer. To say I was upset is an understatement. I wasn't family, but he was my mate, and I loved him dearly. He was my brother from another mother.

For all of us grieving the loss of someone, words never seem to be enough. For a long time after, I often think, I should have said this at his funeral. I should have said that words don't seem to say what we feel in our hearts at the time.

Before we get to the bit he shared for this book, I have included the small tribute I paid to him at his funeral. This was all I could write, but luckily, I knew he understood what I meant.

His mate Pam, "The Pope" as I liked to call her, mainly because she is more spiritual than I ever will be, no matter how many lives I live, read it for me:

I met Rob over 20 years ago. We were both working out of a building in Nottingham, him the handyman and me a drug and alcohol worker. We would often pass in the corridors and have a laugh, him telling me jokes and just passing the day.

Then, one Sunday, I was out for a drive in the peak district and drove back through Belper. Noticing the time, I realised I was close to Belper Spiritualist Church, so calling in for the afternoon service, low and behold, the medium of the day was introduced. It was Mr. Robert Brown, and this was the day I met the real Rob.

He was an incredible medium, but my mediumship was causing me problems. In truth, I needed to trust someone new to push it all into place, and Rob was the lucky one chosen! Well, it took a while, but I got there. I think his job, like most teachers, is just to encourage me, which he truly did.

It was amazing when Rob came to the USA to be with us for a break. We were both like big kids. In all the times he's been here, we've driven up and down the coast, visiting 26 states in all, four times working in eleven of them. The biggest trip we planned was to see New York at Christmas. Nat and I spent two months working out what he would see! Now, if you've watched all the Christmas films about New

York, you would know that the Christmas tree is the ultimate wish on anyone's Christmas list! Yes, it was his biggest wish too.

Well, we made sure that this was going to come true for him no matter what. We spent the day doing incredible stuff, such as the Statue of Liberty, Ground Zero, including hot chocolate every couple of hours. He even met a famous American news reader as she was Christmas shopping in Saks Fifth Avenue store for her famous husband, a morning TV weatherman! The day continued the excitement building, culminating under the Christmas tree at the Rockefeller Plaza, above the ice-skating rink. He loved every second; it was one of the biggest ticks on his bucket list!

Oh, one quick story about food and our travels. We took him to New Orleans where the food is different—good, but different for a couple of lads from the UK! I'm pretty good at trying most things, but Rob! We starved for most of the day until we got to IHOP, (International House of Pancakes), where he promptly ordered fries and eggs. We nearly killed him that day!!

The one thing I can tell you about Rob and the USA, is that everyone he met, everyone he met loved him. I was asked constantly by everyone, including emails from groups where he had done talks about the other love of his life "Aura-Soma," when is Rob coming back?

I could go on for chapter after chapter, telling you stories about our travels here and in the UK. I will save them for another time. For me, it has been an incredible pleasure and an extraordinary experience knowing Rob—all from a meeting 20 years ago in a Spiritualist Church one Sunday afternoon in Belper.

I miss him every day because he was my best friend in this world. I love him as a brother, but it was so much more than that. It's going to take me a long time to get over this, and I know I will not be alone when I say this. For those who knew him, we all know that we have lost someone who gave us love and support. He loved us for being ourselves. He didn't ask me for anything, and I never needed to be someone else when I was with Rob. I was me, and he was himself.

I still get texts from people who talk about him and emails to this day asking, "Can we book Rob for a talk the next time he is in the USA?"

This was the original bit in the book he wrote for me a few years ago. Enjoy!

We all have an aura. It's part of our energy system or electric field that the body uses to exist on this plane, and it is all around us. Everyone has one; we can't exist here without it.

THE HUMAN AURA

The aura is an energy field that surrounds and interpenetrates the physical body. This protective field filters out many of the undesirable energies we encounter and attracts energies that are either needed or desirable. It allows spiritual and psychological interaction with the physical body via structures called chakras. It does this by bringing energy from the environment into the chakras while also dispelling unwanted energies outward. Changes that take place in this energy field can manifest as mental, emotional, or spiritual disturbances, and if left unchecked, may result in physical illness.

The human conscious manifests itself on the various levels or bodies that comprise the aura. Each of us creates our own magnetic atmosphere (aura) that unfailingly reveals the nature of our dispositions, temperament, character, and well-being. This atmosphere acts like an antenna—receiving information and sending out messages—which can be 'read' via the seven standard chakras. Each chakra (save one, the sacral chakra) connects with one layer of the aura. The sacral chakra connects with three layers: the electromagnetic field, the etheric body, and the emotional body.

THE DIFFERENT LAYERS/BODIES WITHIN THE AURA

The Physical Body: This is the most tangible manifestation of consciousness. Its function is to be aware of the here and now; that is, to be conscious of the everyday things we do — walking, talking, eating, etc. Connected with the base chakra and resonating at the frequency of red light, the physical body's main role is that of physical survival.

The Electromagnetic Field: Immediately adjacent to the physical body is the electromagnetic field. This resonates at the higher end of the red wavelength and corresponds with the colour coral. The function of this field is to filter out negative energies or influences which may otherwise harm the physical body.

The Etheric Body: The next level of the aura is the etheric body. This level acts as a template for the physical body and has the appearance of an energy matrix. It is where the chakras are located, and the consciousness expresses itself through the physical sensations of pain and pleasure. The etheric body also acts as the gateway for the soul to pass into and out of the physical body.

The Emotional Body: As you would imagine, the emotional body is where we store and experience emotions. This level of the aura is like a 'super body.' It encompasses the electromagnetic field and the etheric body, with all three sharing the sacral chakra and resonating at the frequency of orange light.

The Mental Body: The mental body is the next level of the aura; its function is to teach us self-knowledge.

The mental body, as its name implies, reflects the state of our conscious mind, our logic, intellect, and our active thought processes. It shapes our reality and reflects the state of our mental health. Being the constructor or builder of reality, it reflects the ability through which we develop our learning and personality. This body connects with the solar-plexus chakra and resonates at the frequency of yellow light.

The Astral Body: The astral body acts as the bridge between the physical world and the spiritual realm. It contains all the previously mentioned bodies and extends some sixteen to twenty inches (40–50 cm) from the physical body. The astral body is the place where we dream and where we astral travel in order to experience other levels of spiritual existence. It connects with the heart chakra and resonates at the frequency of green light.

The Higher Mental Body: The higher mental body connects with memories and thought processes. It is the repository for all our memories forgotten, remembered, or pushed aside. It is the storehouse of the present and all possible futures. This body connects with the throat chakra and resonates at the frequency of blue light.

The Celestial Body: The next level of the aura is the celestial body. This is where our higher consciousness expresses itself through clairvoyance and clairaudience, and where we express our intuition at a higher level. By listening to this higher intuition, we can make our journey through life much simpler and far more rewarding. The celestial body connects with the brow chakra and resonates at the frequency of royal blue light.

The Causal/Ketheric Body: The last and highest level of the aura is the causal or Ketheric body. This is where the soul communicates with the conscious mind via the subconscious mind of the mental body. The causal body is also where consciousness expresses itself in higher knowledge or belief systems. It connects with the crown chakra. The energies within this body spin at very high frequencies and resonate at the colour of violet.

Again, there is so much more information out there so, again, research and remember this is just a brief explanation.

CHAPTER 14:

CHAKRAS

THERE IS AN amazing amount of information about how the chakra system works within the body and what they do. There are some amazing books and websites, so research, research, and research. We have an entire chakra system and an array of emotions flowing through each one. I have included a brief description of each chakra or energy centre, and the following will give you a look at how they sit in the etheric body. As they work, they allow energy to flow through every one of us. To get a complete understanding of how they work and how to work with them in your spiritual journey, you will need to research this subject! I'm not an expert, but if you have unfinished emotional work, it will almost certainly stand out and show up in your body in ways such as stress and tiredness. It will eventually lead to blockages in one or more energy centres or chakras, and if not cleared, it can lead to illness within the body.

As an example, a blockage can be brought on in the throat chakra or *Vishuddha*. If you have been through any emotional problem where you have been unable to say what you want and be heard (which is very important to us all), it will start showing up as a sore throat, a tickly cough, and then sinus and throat infections. For some of us, it can lead to thyroid problems! It really is important to gain an understanding of how the chakras work and how the energy flows around and within us. Understanding how stress can manifest in our bodies and the auric field is also a good idea.

Here is a brief look at the seven main ones that we use in opening up and closing down to do our work. I have included Hindu names and where they sit in the Etheric body.

Base or Root Chakra (Sanskrit name: *Muladhara*)

The base, also known as the root chakra, is red in colour and located at the base of the spine or tailbone in the back and the pubic bone at the front. This energy centre holds the basic survival, security, and safety needs.

Second: Sacral Chakra (Sanskrit name: *Svadhisthana*)

The sacral chakra is located two inches below the navel and fixed into the spine. It is orange in colour. This centre holds the basic needs for sexuality, creativity, intuition, and self-worth. If we have suffered shock in our lives, it will sit as negativity in this chakra.

Third - Solar Plexus (Sanskrit name: *Manipura*)

The next chakra is known as the solar plexus. It is located two inches below the breastbone, in the centre behind the stomach, and is yellow in colour. Within this chakra, we hold the centre of personal power, passions, impulses, anger, and strength. Most of us will carry upset here, and it is also the centre to which most of us will know if and when something is wrong — or as the saying goes, "I got a nasty feeling in the pit of my stomach," and we all get that from time to time!

Fourth - Heart Chakra (Sanskrit name: *Anahata*)

The heart chakra comes next. This one is located behind the breastbone, in the front and at the back of the spine. It is green in colour. This chakra is known to be the centre for love, compassion, and spirituality. If it is aligned, it helps us learn to love ourselves, allowing us to give and receive love from others.

Fifth - Throat Chakra (Sanskrit name: *Vishuddha*)

The next chakra is the throat. It is located at the centre of the collarbone or just above the clavicle notch. It is the centre of communication, sound, and creativeness through speech and writing, and it is blue in colour.

Sixth - Third Eye (Sanskrit name: *Anja*)

The sixth chakra is referred to as the third eye. It is located above the physical eyes on the centre of the forehead. This chakra is indigo in colour. It is the centre for psychic ability, higher intuition, and the energies of spirit and light.

Seventh - Crown Chakra (Sanskrit name: *Sahasrara*)

The last chakra we will discuss in this book is the Crown. It is located on the top of the skull. A perfect way to understand where this energy will flow is to look at a baby's fontanelle on the top of its head, and you will better understand its location. It is violet in colour. The crown chakra is the centre of our spirituality and enlightenment, and it is our connection to the universe, where we receive truth, energy, and love from the source of all-knowing.

When all the charkas are aligned and healthy, they will sit in a column, enabling energy called the Kundalini to rise from the base of the spine to the top of the head, connecting us to universal love and energy. The Kundalini energy lays dormant in every human being, lying like a coiled serpent in the etheric body at the base of the spine.

The Sanskrit word *Kundalini* means coiled like a snake and is not recognised by medical science. However, if you look at the medical symbol, it is a good representation of the Kundalini, with the snakes on either side of the energy column where the charkas sit in flow.

Like the medical symbol, we have three currents of energy: one up the spine and one to each side, coiling around the spine and each chakra. The energy (Kundalini) can be awakened by teachers (gurus) and meditation, but some of us have a natural awakening experience when we develop spiritually.

The Kundalini energy is our life force. Rising through the body and touching each chakra, it then connects to the Universal energy, the source of all-knowing (God), through and out of the crown chakra. So, for a healthy spiritual journey, work on your chakras and let your Kundalini flow. But please remember that we are not meant to sit with our energy flowing 24/7. Remember to close down!

Also know that each soul can gain information from the universe and accelerate its lessons anytime because of free will. We can all come here with a basic understanding of what we're doing but leave with so much growth by allowing ourselves to be open to possibilities of change within our hearts.

With each new incarnation into life, we use the chakras and have very big moments accessing each energy centre for the lessons being gained as we grow. However, the higher the soul comes in on its journey through life, the further up the chakra system it will work from.

PART VI:

ON BEING A MEDIUM

CHAPTER 15:

WHAT IS A MEDIUM?

"The most mind-blowing fact about psychic mediums is that there are really no mind-blowing facts. We are actually very normal people. Some of us are more outgoing, others more introverted. Many of us are rather boring in our lives, just like people who work in any other profession (with the exception of those who routinely do public demonstration.)"

—LISA LARSON, M.A. Evidential Medium, Animal Communicator/Medium, Tarotist[ix]

A MEDIUM WALKS a fine line between two worlds, this one and the next. When I say they walk, I mean they live in two worlds when working. They live here but occasionally visit with the Spirit World or *heaven*. We could say *heaven comes to see them*.

Hmm, I'm not explaining this well, am I? Let's try this again.

Okay, a medium can talk with people who once lived on earth. These people walked among us and were integral to their family and friends. They have passed into the next space, the Spirit World, or *heaven*. (There, that's better.)

There are many names for life after death, but I know you understand—they are now with God in heaven, or whatever you call the next space, and they are now *pure consciousness* or *pure love*, invisible to the naked eye to most of us here. But for mediums such as you and me (well, in truth, all of us, with a little bit of help), we can see, feel, or hear them. So, a medium is a go-between or link to two worlds. Mediums are travellers in time and love. We get the chance to help people left in this world live again after losing a loved one to death; we get the chance to touch eternity to help people love again. But most of all, we prove that life continues.

Our work is about making a difference. As a trained medium, I work with what I believe to be the Spirit World and interact using mediumship to connect both worlds and thus communicate with the dead... but maybe that's a bit dramatic. Let's just say I talk with real people who have passed over. If you have ever seen the television show *Quantum Leap*, Sam Beckett (played by Scott Bakula) travelled in time and space. We, as mediums, are doing something very similar. We are just not leaping into other people's bodies; it is about us as human beings travelling into love. All mediums are highly sensitive individuals whose heightened sense of awareness can be used to form links between the living and people who have passed over.

Working as an *evidential medium* is about evidence that is recognisable and can be confirmed. This often includes your relationship with the person, including personality traits, physical characteristics, names, and memories. The medium links the Spirit world and the Spirits of the departed to communicate with friends and loved ones still in the physical world on earth. The medium should provide you proof without you offering any information, which can and should be checked and confirmed by you, the *sitter*. A medium provides evidence that life has continued after the body has ceased. Most will have a sense of who they have with them. They are there to prove life and love after death with evidence that can include all sorts of information.

There you go—a bit repetitive, but I think I explained it well!

When I started out wanting to be a medium, no one told me to be careful what I asked for because once I opened the doors, I found it hard to shut them again. There are mediums and teachers out there who say Spirit is great. They will not hurt or bother you, which is true for most, however, if you do not control yourself, you will lose yourself. And if *you* do not get control of working with Spirit, *they* will take control and drive you crazy. It is a fine line between being a medium and being crazy because we walk between two worlds. Remember, asking to be a medium will not always be fun or easy! Just learn who you are and have boundaries for both worlds—"bloody big ones"— and keep yourself safe and sane.

My advice is to always move forward with your work. Keep learning and be proud of what you do. You will not be able to tell everyone that you are a medium or a psychic, or as I like to call myself: "a psychotic medium." But you will be able to acknowledge it to yourself, and that is a big thing.

And of all the things I could advise you to do as you start being a medium, it would be to *trust*. This might be a big ask at the start because you will think you're making a lot of this up, but TRUST, TRUST, and TRUST. What do I mean by that? As you venture on your spiritual journey, you will find that if you want to work with Spirit, you must do just that. It's tough having conversations in your head or talking to people who have passed, people no one else can see or hear but you. You will look strange to most, but you get used to it. And you're not crazy; you just have a fantastic gift.

There will be times when your understanding of others will be sorely tested; just so you know. There are some lovely people out there stuck in pain but there are a few crazies, too! Just try to remember you are only human. With all the glory that goes with that, people can and will drive you crazy. You will also have to live with doubters. People will come to you and tell you they don't believe in you or accuse you of having plants in an audience. You might also give someone incredible evidence only for them to sit there crying, telling you you're terrific. Then, if you give them something they don't remember or can't give them a name, they will refuse to pay you and call you useless.

My advice is to remember to breathe. Be you and take breaks. Try to be centred and deal with the shit the universe throws at you. Most of all, know you are great. And here is the big one: YOU CANNOT SAVE EVERYONE. So always TRUST YOU when it comes to your work.

The resurgence in modern-day mediumship is in part thanks to television and to people like Colin Fry (sadly no longer with us, passed to the Spirit World), Derek Acorah (again, sadly no longer with us, passed to the Spirit World), Mea Dolan, Tony Stockwell, Betty Shine, and Gordon Smith to name but a few in the UK. In the USA, Sylvia Brown (also sadly no longer with us, passed to the Spirit World).

There's John Edward, James Van Praagh, John Holland, Theresa Caputo, and Rosemary Altea (British).

There are mediums from all over the world, such as Deb Webber Kelvin Cruikshank (Australian) and Sue Nicholson (New Zealand but another British-born medium), who are helping us all across the world become aware of our gifts. I know there are incredible mediums in every country who need to be thanked. They have all given us the opportunity to learn and stand up and say, "I am a Medium." I am proud to shout it out!

People will ask if mediums are doing the Devil's work ... HELL NO! Absolutely Not! Legitimate mediums are doing something that can give people closure and the freedom to move on. We offer something that can provide hope and peace, which can make the difference between someone living or taking their own life. We, as mediums, engage with love and light, we engage Spirit.

It's interesting when you look at it: most religions advertise their wears by saying, "Join us. The truth is here." They say there is an afterlife in the Kingdom of Heaven with God; you see it on all church boards. We really don't believe in anything too different from that, except we are blessed with gifts that allow us to engage with that energy, that love. We don't have to wait to die to feel God's love or to realise that our loved ones have passed over to an eternal existence.

Everyone is offered love and light, no matter what we do here, and the universe balances it out with love over time. It's called *karma*. There is no hell—yet again, another lie created by man to keep you in control and following their path like sheep. There is no hell, but we all do a great job of trying to create that here.

Some religions do not understand what we are doing. They believe that what we are undertaking is wrong and proceed to paint us with a tarnished brush because we actually might get people to seek their own truth. For centuries, mediums have been misunderstood and wrongly labelled, but this is often what happens when something that can't be explained is criticized. The truth is, the world remains largely free—though how free it feels often depends on your level of cynicism, and how you view the entanglement between governments and religions, or vice versa.

It's a very strange thing that we were mentioned in the Bible once or twice, the main one being the medium from Endor, which has now been changed to the witch of Endor. I love that people try to live by something created by man, not God. I'll pose a question: if it was God, did he just simply talk to them, appear in front of them, or did he channel it into someone? Surely, that would make that person a medium.

Spiritualism and mediums are given a hard time by most religions, but I am not having a go at any religion in particular. The fact is, we are using natural gifts that we are all born with and freely given to us by God. Yes, the one and only—your God and my God.

The fact of the matter is, we live in peace and do not push our religious beliefs or ourselves onto anyone. We don't knock on doors, and we don't proclaim any other religion to be wrong. We don't threaten anyone with anything. We don't write books or stand in a little box on Sunday, proclaiming that if you don't believe in one deity above another, you will burn in eternal damnation.

What we do is help others understand that life does go on after death and that you don't have to believe in anything unless you want to. All you have to do is be willing to be open to your truth, and if that truth is God and Jesus, Allah, Buddha, or spacemen, then that's fine. Live in peace. And let others live in peace. Stop telling the rest of the world they're going to burn in hell. Yes, I know, I am having a go at a bunch of people. But the thing is, it's getting old and boring! If people want to stay closed in their minds, there isn't much anyone can do for them.

Like any institution, religion has its share of individuals who exploit the vulnerable—taking advantage of trust for personal gain, whether through money, addiction, or worse. Similarly, the world of mediumship is not immune to deception. There are those who prey on the grieving and the hopeful, not from a place of love and light, but from ego and self-interest. These individuals do not represent the true spirit of the work—they distort it. We mediums can face ridicule and scepticism from many places. We just don't see everything the same way, and it would not do for us all to follow the same path. We each have a personal journey of discovery and unfoldment, and there are many lessons in the belief in a God and following a path, whether right or wrong. If we didn't, we wouldn't need to be here.

We believe in God, and we do not judge anyone for following their path to him, so please don't judge us on our path. We are all energy, and Spirit is that living energy on another plain. Who says we can't see or talk to them? God did not make that rule. MAN DID!

Finally, we are not saying our religion is better than any other one, so please let us be!

Sorry, I tried not to rant but I've been getting this crap for years, so this was my turn to stand in the pulpit.

I do love being asked if we mediums believe in God. Yes, of course we do. As spiritualists, we believe in God. Our church services on a Sunday are just like most other churches. We pray to a Him or Her God, and we sing hymns. It is a normal church service. (There are those out there who will say it's not normal, you are talking to the dead. Well, in truth, they are more alive than we are here.)

When working in any church service in the UK or USA, we respect what we say. God is a very personal thing to each of us, and it is not for anyone here on this planet to tell us how to live or who to worship. The sooner every religion and every government down here understands this, the sooner we will all be free of the shackles that tie us down and keep us in place to be controlled.

I have come through mainstream religion, and for the most, I'm not too badly scarred! I just find it so hard to fathom why we were all taught as children that God was such a nasty, wrathful God. In reality, He or She is loving, caring, compassionate, and truly wants the best for us. Just ask my wife!

"Yes. Most mediums and psychics I know believe in a higher spiritual being, and depending on their initial religious upbringing, that often dictates who that higher spiritual being is. My religious background is Catholic, and I know that when we I pray, I still have to start with "Dear Lord" because that was how I always started to pray when I was younger. It is the most comfortable space for me."

—NATALIE MITCHELL

Getting back to the question at hand, "Do mediums believe in God?" When I first started doing services, I was told that we could mention other religions and deities when doing philosophy in a church service. As working mediums, we have learnt to adapt to where we are and be very respectful of what we say when doing any kind of service in a Spiritualist Church in the UK or USA.

We encourage everyone to talk about their beliefs respectfully in any of our classes. I love to ask students to stand up and teach us about God or Spirit in their own words, plus their journey to how they found themselves and Him or Her.

"When the power of love overcomes the love of power, the world will know peace."

—JIMI HENDRIX

CHAPTER 16:

CAN I BE A MEDIUM?

THE SHORT ANSWER is yes! There are many natural-born mediums, but some of us need to have it awakened in us. Once it starts to become more open within you, seeking guidance and direction through classes with good teachers is more conducive. No one can make you a medium. All a teacher can do is bring out your potential by making you work differently. It's actually about you and Spirit discovering which methods work best for you both, helping you to strengthen your contact and bond. For some people, becoming a medium can take a long time with a lot of work and perseverance from both sides. In truth, it will eventually come down to one thing and one thing only: TRUST. Without it, you will be waiting a long time to move forward with your mediumship. So, do yourself a favour at the start of your unfoldment, because I promise this will save you a lot of trouble in the long run: TRUST!

We are all gifted in some way, some more than others, depending on what you've come in here to do with your life. But most of us will have amazing intuition and say things from time to time that will mean so much to another person. They may look at you like you are crazy, but you're tapping into Spirit guides or their guides and loved ones and you don't even know it. The reality is, it's something we have used for most of our lives, and if we look deep enough, we will find it.

Most will not even realise they're tapping into this, and it won't matter to them. They will just continue with life and do it from a natural place. However, many will come looking for people like me to help them use their gifts more as they start their spiritual journey. That doesn't mean to say they will stay and become mediums. It simply means they are open to possibilities. Not everybody wants to become crazy like me and stand on a platform, giving messages, or doing personal and private readings.

I think one of the funniest things I say, and it's so true, is for women. They have what is commonly called *women's intuition*. I personally call this a *bullshit detector*. We men know that if we try and get around it, women will mostly see what we're trying to do, no matter what! There is no way it's going to work. You are not getting around their BS detector. LOL! But most of you reading this have had a "gut" feeling, which is your intuition at work. The choice you must make is how far you take that gift. For most of us, intuition is just another muscle you need to work on.

The majority of people in the world, when born, will have *gifts*. Most stop using them as they go through life, but there is a time when something happens that will flip it open, even if it's for a brief moment.

Then they go back to their lives and shut it down without even acknowledging this part of the naturalness of their bodies.

There can also be times when the doors float open or feel like they have completely smashed open because of something that has happened in our lives that makes us question who we are. I've said before that people will come looking for answers and either want to open more and play or want help shutting down. As mediums and teachers, we're here to help. I never force anybody to do something they're not comfortable doing. And if I can help them understand how to quiet the noise down or help them walk away, I will.

My only advice to everybody is to always, always acknowledge *you* and do what is right for *you*, not for anybody else—for *you*. That's what you're here for: to be you.

That said, anyone can learn to be a medium. However, as with the above answer, it takes time. It just doesn't happen overnight. If you are open to all of these ideas and allow yourself to grow into something incredible, the simple answer is yes, anybody can do this. You have to take your time, believe in yourself, and remember you're not crazy.

To find a teacher, in the UK, ask at your local Spiritualist Church. In the USA, go to a Metaphysical Church or shop. Finding a teacher is like finding a needle in a haystack. Again, with anything important in life, do yourself a big favour: *research, research,* and *research.* A teacher is a very personal guide. They can be enlightening, frightening, or damn right annoying if you don't get who you want, so do the research.

Teachers should be there to guide you. They cannot make you a medium or psychic. What they can do is help you learn to trust and believe in yourself. They should also be teaching you basic things, such as *opening up* and, more importantly, *closing down* to protect yourself. This is a practice I cannot stress enough. It should be worked on daily. Unless you want to be grumpy a lot of the time, close down.

In the world of mediumship, there are some very gifted and worthy people working and teaching. It was a struggle for me to find teachers, but I did eventually get there. I have had some incredible teachers and friends. In this work, as in life, there are some ego-driven, pig-headed morons to be found! These people generally have their own agenda: to make others look small and take them apart without the slightest bit of concern, which leads to harm. Why do they do this? For no other reason than they can. Or worse, they believe they are right and are connected to Spirit.

They may pull you down and hold you back because of fear that you will become a better medium. They may abuse you because they believe they are superior and are trying to get you out of their class. I've been there and had this done to me several times. When people attend my classes, they are encouraged to be the best they want to be—not battered and left to try and pick themselves up off the floor. So, here's a very good warning for those who are stepping into a class for the first time: please remember everything you have learned in the world so far. Inauthentic people claiming to be spiritual are really just scumbags, and a scumbag in my world is a scumbag!

It's important to recognise them. Their egos are rampant. It is the same behaviour seen in regular society, but they call themselves spiritual. In truth, this is worse because they claim to be doing their work in the name of God! If it sounds like I have had some bad experiences, it's because I have. PLEASE *research, research,* and *research* again. If you're not happy or don't feel that you have clicked with the teacher, find somebody else. There are many times when people come to my class, and they don't like me. I am okay with that. I laugh, joke, have fun, and swear a lot. I do not have an ego about my work. I'm here to help people, not put them down.

And when you find a worthy teacher, how often you take lessons will depend on the time you have available and your daily schedule. But if you could, try to go once a week or every other week to start to build your relationship with your guide, Spirit, teacher, and most importantly, yourself.

You can also find *development* or *open circles*. A development or open circle in mediumship is a supportive, structured group session where people of all levels (beginners to experienced) gather to practice and enhance their psychic and mediumship abilities in a safe, non-judgmental space, often led by an experienced medium. Participants meditate, share spiritual insights, practice giving and receiving messages from spirit, learn techniques, and connect with a like-minded community to grow their connection to the spirit world.

These circles build up your energy, help you understand how the process works, and sense the signals and signs we receive. The natural gifts we had have to be switched back on. Instead of just talking to Spirit, we must learn a new language, with signs, signals, stops, and starts. This is a lifetime's work and will always change if you want to be the best.

People think that doing a reading and working with Spirit is not hard. I can tell you from my experience that it is very draining. Working and trying to manage your energy can be a lifetime's work in itself. If you're lucky, and get a good teacher, you can learn to protect yourself. Classes are not just about learning to be a medium. They are about learning how amazing you are, too.

If you're still with me, I'll bet your next question is, "How long should I train, how long should I sit in a circle before I give readings?" No amount of time is set in stone, and it varies from person to person. What I recommend, though, is once it has been established that your readings in the development circle have been accurate for a few months, and you feel confident, start to practise with more people outside your friends and family.

I was guided by a friend, Marianne Hope Clarke. She said, "Why not go along and raise money for your church or favourite charity, charge a nominal fee, and split it between you both?" It's still great advice, and I offer it to my students.

Of course, all of this is down to you. The way you will know will be through trust and courage. In the circles I work with, I help people start to do this within six months. It's also a great way for them to work with me so I know how to encourage them more with different tasks and tools. Garre Liana, who has been with me for a couple of years and is now a professional reader, still attends classes from time to time if she has something she needs to work on or wants to try something new. It is not an overnight thing. It is a slow process for some and involves learning more about themselves first. You can't just jump in at the deep end; well, you can but it will help you more to attend a class for a while, if only to build up your confidence up.

A good teacher will help you learn to work with the voice (Spirit) at first. It may be working with oracle cards, psychometry, crystals, your psychic ability, or mediumship. These are all gifts a teacher will help you cultivate over a few years. I have been doing this for a long time but still attend classes with my mentors. I am always looking to improve my work and myself so, for me, I will always be learning.

IMPORTANT:

You cannot work twenty-four hours a day, seven days a week. It is not physically possible, and let me tell you, I have tried! You must have personal time and remember you are also here to live your life. You can help people all day long and they will still want more. So, make sure you are not at the beck and call of everyone, and learn to live as well.

You must take time each day to remember what you want from this. We are all here to continue our journey, but you must be in touch with your heart, and remember who you are.

CHAPTER 17:

OPEN & CLOSED

IN MEDIUMSHIP, "OPENING" means intentionally becoming receptive to spirit communication, shifting consciousness to a higher vibration or different reality for connection. "Closing" is vital, it's disengaging, grounding, and protecting oneself by shutting down that connection, preventing overwhelming spiritual energy or unwanted entities from lingering, ensuring a return to normal physical reality and mental well-being. It's a skill, like turning on/off a faucet, to manage spiritual sensitivity and maintain balance.

And there are at least two different ways to look at how we protect ourselves or "stay open."

THE FIRST WAY TO LOOK AT IT

Since I moved to the USA, I have encountered this in most places: people think they are gaining something from being open all the time and feel if they close down, they will miss something spiritually. Let's get this clear: You will not miss anything—but you may become depressed, tired, full of emotional pain and sorrow from other people's energy, and eventually sick.

We are energy receivers/transmitters, producing an electric field of energy. For example, it's like this: you walk into a shop having had a great start to your day. You got up, the kids were on time, and everything was going your way. Tonight, your other half is taking you out. It's date night, you're going to your favourite restaurant, and life is great.

You stop for some stuff at the shop, pick up what you want, and then stand in the queue to pay. The person in front of you has had a bad morning. Their partner has pissed them off, someone just crashed into their car, and they must go to work for a boss who's a jerk and only cares about making the next dollar for himself. You stand behind them, and their emotions are raging. Within minutes, you feel down, drained, and upset. You haven't closed yourself down, so you are now open to a psychic invasion/attack! You are being attacked and don't even realise how. What is happening? Remember, with all energy, it moves and flows. Your aura pulls in emotion. The good is transmitted out and the bad is pulled in. Before you know it, you have a complete exchange of emotions and energy. They leave the shop in a good mood, and you leave feeling like shit!

This happens to us every day and in any place. At first, you just feel tired and perceive it to be just one of those days, then one of those weeks, and then on to months. Eventually, who knows what it turns into? That's why I teach closing down. (Most teachers have their way and show you how to do this; there are many other ways to keep us secure spiritually while on this planet.) I go through it in every class, before we finish, to get everyone into a habit of protecting and keeping the aura and chakras clear.

What you are doing is protecting yourself from other people's stuff, but you are also setting an intention for everything and everyone around you! You are saying, "I am not open. I am closed for business to piss off and annoy someone else, Spirit or human alike!" A lot of teachers don't believe in this but it's something that has served me well. The next chapter will take you through it.

THE SECOND WAY TO LOOK AT IT

If we are open to change, are we stopping our emotional growth—something we came here to grow and learn about—by closing down? Is this a disservice to what we want to achieve here with our spirituality? I think it's fair to say we grow from every life lesson, and our chakras are built to give us a complete sense of each other and the world around us. For example, if we look at just one of our energy centres, the *heart chakra*, it is the focus and conciseness of love for others and ourselves. We navigate the emotional world of being human, feeling love and a sense of balance by allowing this energy centre to flow as we move through life. So, does it make sense to protect it and keep it closed?

The reality of this world has become so harsh for everyone who wants to win or be right. Just one example: people are attacking us in our own homes through a computer. Adults and children are being bullied for having an opinion on some of the most trivial things. They lose confidence and belief in themselves. So, they lock the doors, stay in a self-made prison, and never get the courage to experience life or intimacy with anyone again.

This is just one illustration of how we hurt each other. If I were to look at love, there would be an entirely different book of what we do to each other just for LOVE.

I suppose the question is, should we close down or stay open? My personal feeling is that we need to learn to use our energy in a way that we can close it down and open it to the world around us as we flow with life. We are living through times of great stress. We each face new challenges every day, and I think this is one thing we must learn, and that is to have healthy boundaries.

It's easy for me to write this and you to read it but putting it into practice is another thing altogether. The truth is we are here to learn in love and pain! At the end of the day this is down to you.

But if you learn how to control your energy while remembering to be open to life, love, and living, you really can't go that wrong.

Final word, when I speak of "closing down," I mean gathering your energy in, cover it with a cloak, bubble, suit of armour, ball of mirrors be creative. Drawing it inward to rest within the sanctuary of your own space. We can never truly close—not until we slip the bonds of the body, and even then, a trace of us lingers, echoing in the unseen.

EACH OF US needs to learn a simple technique for closing down, and what suits you will work best.

First, learn where all your chakras are. There is a lot of information about how they work and what they do, including a piece here in this book. Just to run through them, we have:

1. base

2. sacral

3. solar plexus

4. heart

5. throat

6. third eye

7. and finally, the crown.

There are some really good books and websites out there, but as with everything, be sure to research, research, and research some more to make sure you are getting good information.

Second, once you know where all the chakras sit within the body, I want you to picture a door—any kind of door. It can be wood or metal, that is your choice. Now that you have your door, visualise your hand as that door so you are doing something physical. Place it over each chakra. Start at the base and move up to each chakra, touching and closing each centre, including the crown chakra.

The next bit is about sealing in everything tightly, reflecting and transforming negativity away from you with love and light.

Back to visualising, place yourself in a white ball of light sealed all around your physical body. Then surround that ball with another ball of light, this time making it pink, but again sealing yourself in all the way around your physical body. Finally, place yourself in a ball of mirrors, (picture a disco ball), the mirrors facing outward and sealing you in completely.

You should now be set with all your chakras protected behind closed doors, surrounded by a protective white and pink light, and finally, reflecting mirrors facing outward. Now ask your God, Goddess, guides, and helpers to keep you safe until you open up to work again.

At first, it may take a couple of minutes to get the hang of doing this, but I can promise you it is worth it in the long run. Suppose anyone anywhere is sending negativity toward you. It will be sent back without you even doing anything because you chose white light (it is pure white light), pink light (which is pure pink love), and mirrors (which will reflect whatever is sent toward you). Know it will be sent back with love, not negativity.

Chapter 18:

On Working With Spirit

WHEN STARTING TO train as a medium, one of the first things I was taught was to *tune into Spirit*. It's something I still take time to do. Yes, there are times when I have to just get on with it, but I try and give myself at least five minutes. It will make a world of difference to your work, and whether it's five minutes or twenty, attuning to yourself and Spirit will help strengthen you over the years as a professional medium.

Remember…

If you are thinking, *you* are questioning.

If you are questioning, *you* are doubting.

If you are doubting, *you* are putting *you* in.

And if you are putting *you* in this, it will involve your own personal stuff and not the clients, thus giving everyone a strange sitting!

Try to use self-reflexivity as a tool during your work. It's an ability to look thoughtfully at oneself. It can be challenging sometimes, but it helps to ask, "What is the impact of this reading bringing up for me, and what experiences have I been through that are similar to the clients and coming out in this reading?" Believe me, it will stop you from becoming involved in your client's stuff and save you time and money going to see a counsellor yourself.

BELOW IS A list of information you should look for when doing a mediumship reading. It's a list that makes up what it is to be a human. It's not fully complete, but if you're going to train as a medium, you may find this helpful and practical at the start, so you get used to looking for certain things.

You should get all this information from Spirit, not by asking questions of the person in front of you. If you're asking questions of the person, why don't you just ask them to do their own reading and pay you? You're ripping them off, and you're not there to rip ANYBODY off. You're there to prove that life goes on.

As a reader if you use this list without asking questions, you should be able to get decent evidence from each Spirit that comes in.

SPIRITUAL EVIDENCE: IDENTIFY–RECOGNIZE

The best evidence is that which can be checked and confirmed. It's proof of life first and then the message.

- Gender: How does the person identify, and what are you intuitively picking up?

- Names: What is their full name, pet names, and nicknames?

- Relationship: Are they a father, mother, brother, sister, child, or stepfamily? Do they have a maternal or paternal link? What are some family details?

- Shape or Size: Are they slim, well-built, medium-built, or large-built?

- Posture: Do they stand upright, bent forward, like someone from the military, or slouch?

- Height: Are they taller than you or shorter than you? What is their approximate height?

- Hair: What is its colour, length, amount, or style? Or are they bald?

- Face: What are some distinguishing features, such as close-set eyes, eye colour, the shape of their eyes or face, nose shape, mouth shape, facial hair (like a moustache or beard), birthmarks, or moles?

- Conditions: What are their illnesses, aches, and pains?

- Personality: Describe as much as you can.

- Children: How many? If any, are they male or female?

- Dates: What are their birthdays or anniversaries (think weddings, births, deaths, etc.)?

- Where They Lived: What's their address, town, city, or country?

- Memories: What are some memories of shared times?

- Lifestyle Habits: Do they smoke or not smoke? Do they drink or not drink?

- Occupation: What's their occupation?

- Hobbies: What do they do for fun (sports, knitting, motor racing, horses, etc.)?

- Clothes: What type of clothing and shoes do they wear? Do they wear hats, belts, or suspenders?

- Food Likes and Dislikes: Do they like meat, potatoes (chips), vegetables, cakes, puddings, sweets, chocolate, etc.?

- The reason for Spirit being here

- Finally, what is the message?

Use this list as a prompt, it is not the be all, end all. Use it to train yourself to be more observant. *The best evidence is in the unusual, so keep and trust your contact.* Don't try to explain or add more than you are given. It is the recipient's evidence, not yours.

IT IS AMAZING how many people tell me they wake up in the middle of the night at the same time. The short and simple answer is that you have relaxed your mind, and it is now clear and can be easily communicated with. It's like Spirit sees a bright light and starts communication that wakes you up.

I have two words that need to be remembered: *control* and *boundaries*. When it comes to taking back our sleep, it's about taking back control. When you first start connecting to Spirit or vice versa, you are given all these beautiful gifts and then you start the lessons. They let you see and hear them, and you start to get glimpses of what's coming up in the future. This is fine and good, but to me, lesson one is about control and who is in control.

On that side, we have Spirit, and on this side is us! Now, remember that because it will save a lot of time and trouble in the long run. Control and boundaries are the two words to remember.

We as humans are very inquisitive. We like attention, and when something comes calling, we want to learn, learn, and learn now. Learning's fine, but we have to take control when it comes to our health and sleep. If you have kids and have to drive the car the following day to take them to school or anywhere else, you can't do it half asleep.

If Spirit can talk to someone and get a message across, they will. Let's stop right there. Let me point this out to you: they are in the next world. They don't need to eat or sleep. My advice is to tell them that you would like to talk to them at a regular time of the day. It's like making an appointment to sit in the energy and the power, and you're going to talk to them.

I have watched people and thought about this hard for a long time. We have guides, and they are supposed to help. But this is *our* life and choices.

Visits at night are a great opportunity for us all to learn how to say no. It's one of the hardest things for some of us to do. Our guides want us to stand up and say NO. They allow this intrusion in the middle of the night to bug us, and yes, it will bug you until you say NO.

The control on this side is knowing when to say no. You wouldn't allow your friend to pop over for a chat at 3:33 am. No. Setting time aside to work with Spirit in the day is like setting time to spend with your friends.

Practice the close-down we've already discussed, and if that doesn't work, tell them to get out and leave you alone. Say it in the way you want to be heard. Make sure they get your message: you need to sleep. You may have to go to work or drive the kids to school, or you could have an exam the next day. It doesn't matter. You have to live and be aware of what you are doing in the daytime. TAKE CONTROL.

Now, admittedly, this doesn't happen to everybody. If it doesn't, then consider yourself lucky. But if this is happening to you, please pay attention. And before you start to worry that they will not come back in the day, don't. They will be back. As my teacher Rob used to say, "They don't invest time on people, then walk away." It's in both side's interest that you rest from time to time.

WHEN I FIRST started to train as a medium, I asked one of my teachers, "Why do I hear ringing in my ears?" The answer I got back was, "They (Spirit) are drilling a hole in your head." What she meant was that Spirit is tuning you into another frequency. If you had a radio and wanted to pick up a different station, you would turn the dial to tune into it. Well, in truth, that's all that is happening. With the help of your guides, you are tuned up to receive a better signal.

> **Important:** If you have been getting constant noise in your ears, please first go to your doctor to make sure you do not have tinnitus, an ear infection, or any other medical issue.

I FEEL STRONGLY, as a medium, about walking up to strangers and giving them messages. Natalie even gives a 20-minute speech on this topic whenever she can. We have both contributed to this answer and, as you will see from what follows, it is something that annoys each of us. The answer is: *never, ever!* It is simply unprofessional, unethical, and wrong. We have a term (in truth, we have a few) for people who can't keep control of their egos, mouths, or gifts and approach others to give messages in the street, shops, bars, or anywhere in public. We call them *leaky mediums!*

Just so you know, when someone is doing this for television, ALL participants have been approached prior to the show and asked to sign a release to appear on camera before the working medium talks to them.

Mediumship is not a party trick that you get out to impress your friends. It is not something to use to let your ego out to play. We have heard horror stories of people just walking up to someone and giving him or her a so-called message from a loved one, potentially causing more harm than good.

The problem is this:

You DO NOT know the person standing in front of you.

You DO NOT know where he/she is emotionally in life.

You DO NOT know who the person from the Spirit World is if you are in a public place, and there is a lot of negativity on the streets.

Finally, you DO NOT know how the person is going to take the information you are about to BLURT out to them.

Even if the Spirit persists in bugging you to speak to the person in front of you, don't do it. DO NOT ever believe that you have the right to approach anyone and give a reading. You do not have the right. I'll repeat this: YOU DO NOT HAVE THE RIGHT!

You are playing with fire.

You are playing with emotions.

And you are not working ethically!

Gain control over your mediumship, gain control over your EGO, and gain control over you. I'll repeat it again: *this is not a party trick that you get out to impress anyone.* If you think it is okay or you regularly walk up to people in the street, in shops, in bars, or anywhere in public, then refrain from doing this for the ethical mediums in this world who would never dream of doing this.

Please stop and think about the person standing in front of you, going home with a message you provided from someone who could have raped, beaten, or completely screwed up their lives. Put yourself in their shoes and imagine how it would feel if *you* were approached by someone you don't know and had your innermost secrets pulled out in the middle of a public place.

The reason ethics are so close to Natalie's heart is that she was actually told a story by a so-called "medium" in one of her classes and was horrified that this medium would tell a story and not be embarrassed or see the insensitivity of her actions. Natalie truly believes she was told this story to prove the point as to why we NEVER walk up to strangers and give them messages. Here's her story:

A "medium" was at a party and had a Spirit telling her to go to a young woman standing on the other side of the room and tell her he was sorry. The "medium" did not know this woman at all. They were complete strangers to each other.

With no regard for anyone, the situation, or the location, this "medium" walked up to the girl—who was standing with several other people—and proceeded to tell her that she was a medium and there was a guy named "Tom" (not the real name) with her and that he said he was sorry. The girl looked at the medium with sheer disgust and asked her how she knew "Tom." Again, the medium stated that he was in Spirit, and he wanted her to tell this young woman he was sorry. The woman, in tears and clearly upset, said, "I don't care if he is dead, I don't care if he is sorry. He raped me and ruined my life."

Because the "medium" was too wrapped up in her own ego and her need to show she could do this, she completely disregarded who the communicator from the Spirit World could be. She never established the relationship the Spirit had with this complete stranger. And as you can see, there were obvious consequences: an emotional reaction in the middle of a party.

My question is, what about the things we *didn't* see? What happens if this woman had been going for therapy and was starting to move through this situation in a positive direction and now it was all thrown back in her face? What if the people she was with had no idea this had happened to her, and now she is placed in a situation where this personal trauma was shared by a stranger?

As mediums and psychics, we are blessed with a gift that, when we are invited in, often helps heal the soul and move people into a place of peace and comfort. This is a double-edged sword though – **if we are not invited in,** we can cause problems and bring up issues that people may or may not be ready to handle.

As a working medium, I have literally done readings where people have had every kind of imaginable thing happen to them in life, and the Spirit has come through to apologize or to help the person heal. I stopped the reading, had a conversation with the person, and asked if they wished to continue. Do they want me to ask the person in Spirit to step back or would they like to stop the reading?

This is called ethics. Learn about it before you blurt out people's personal lives in public, damaging and hurting them further. Learn to work professionally. Have your own personal ethics where you take people's feelings and pain into consideration.

However, after all of that, if you still want to be someone who gets out your mediumship and special gifts at a party or in the middle of a shop—to let your damn ego out and show people how damn clever you are—then my advice is to stop! Don't do it. Shut the FUCK up! Stop giving real mediums a bad name and making us all look like fucking NUTTERS!!!

The soapbox is put away and the rant over... until we get letters. And when we do, we are going to answer them the same. So, if you are considering writing to us, know this is how we feel and we are not going to change our minds!

I HAVE WATCHED the argument over how much a medium should be paid go back and forth for years, about charging money for readings. Some people believe this to be a God-given gift, so we mustn't charge. As spiritual people, why do we feel we should be the poorest people out there, and why do we not think we are providing a service that requires an exchange or payment?

When I first started going for readings, I was quite happy to pay someone to speak to my loved ones to get closure and peace. It was something of a joke to my family and friends that I would ever think of going to see a medium, even to the suggestion that I was going to speak with people doing "the Devil's work," which I have answered quite well in this book! But I kept going and paying for it. It was something I accepted. I looked at it like this: it was an exchange of energy.

When I first started doing readings, I charged £5 (about $7.50). Then, after a while, I asked for £10 (about $15), and finally, a lot longer after, I got up to £25 (roughly $37-$50). I was happy I was providing service and learning my trade. I was also getting paid for my time, and it was how much I valued my time then!

Take the following: we think nothing of encouraging children to practice and use their gifts as baseball players, premier footballers, sprinters, and long jumpers. Even college kids are getting paid to take their God-given gifts to a particular establishment. Nobody thought it was strange when they wanted to play their favourite sport every day to be the best and try to get to the top in their chosen field. (No one is saying people haven't worked hard to achieve great success. The sports stars are paid astronomical fees every week for their chosen sports. How often have you heard people describe these gifts as God-given?)

I have spent my money to advance my gifts. I didn't wake up one morning and think, "Hey, I'm a medium." I, like most mediums and psychics, have invested in myself and continue to do so. I've attended classes (development circles) for a long time, and if I want to go to AFC, I have to pay for it.

Like most people in this work, I have to find the money to live, as well as to pay for my education. In my continued professional development, I have and continue to pay for schooling in counselling, healing, coaching, hypnotherapy, Reiki, etc. They have all cost me a lot of money, but in truth, I make full use of them in my work so, for me, it's been money well spent.

I value my time and the amount of money I have had to pay to get this far. Believe me, I am not charging astronomical fees for any of the services that I offer; I am just putting a price on my time. I don't charge for my gifts; you pay for my time.

I do this full-time, and anyone who is a plumber, electrician, or does any kind of building work doesn't do it for free. No one ever argues after they have fixed a leak or electrical sockets on the wall. They get paid for the service provided.

I don't want to argue with anybody. I just want to say, *value you* and go with your conscience. We offer a service that's very important to someone who has lost a child, a husband, a wife, a mother, or a father. It's a chance to get closer. If you disagree, please keep it to yourself. This argument is getting old, and so am I!

CHAPTER 19:

HOW TO CLEAN A LIVING SPACE OF A SPIRIT OR NEGATIVITY

"Our home is an extension of our personality. Our physical and emotional comfort is often based on the question. 'Do you know your home?'"

—TERRY AND NATALIA O'SULLIVAN, *Soul Rescuers: A 21st Century Guide to the Spirit World*

MANY COACHES WILL talk about cleaning out your physical space, which will help clear your mind. The reason I teach people to do this is because it's about you taking control of YOUR living space. Remember, it's YOUR living space!

I have been shown several ways and combined them for most situations over the years. This is long, but it's not complicated. It will help you, and in the end, you will find your way of doing this, which will work just as well.

IMPORTANT:

Always remember, before any energy clearings, never, ever start on the outside first. **You are going to cleanse from the inside out.** If you do the outside first, you will be trapping any negativity inside. So again, you are cleaning from the inside to the out.

TOOLS YOU WILL NEED:

- **Salt.** It doesn't matter which sort: cooking, rock, or sea salt. Salt is a purifier and cleanser and is mentioned in the Bible as such.

- **Water.** Use holy water, if you can. (Don't worry, I will tell you how to make it.) Holy water is a sacrament for protection against evil, and common among world religions.

- **Eucalyptus oil (and hot water).** A cleanser purifier, when this oil is mixed with hot water, it allows for easy breathing and cleaner, purer air.

- **Safety glasses.** These will protect your eyes from the oil and hot water.

- **White sage.** Sage has been used for thousands of years in Native American tradition and by shamans throughout the world to cleanse you or a space. When buying sage, remember you will be inhaling the smoke into your lungs, so it is best to buy it from a reputable dealer, as there can be substances or unnatural additives added.

- **A bird's feather.** Feathers are used because they come from certain birds believed to have wisdom and medicine power.

- **A bell or singing bowl.** The bell and singing bowl create a harmonic vibration. They can heal and cleanse you and the living space.

- **Two spray bottles.** Spray water bottles can help direct water into the corner or space.

TO GET STARTED:

Before you begin, line everything up on a kitchen counter, table, or altar, if you have one. Go into the silence asking your God, guides, angels, and helpers to step in and help you with this work. Say a prayer of your choosing, asking for each tool to be blessed with love and light, and to be used in harmony with your God's truth and will. With this exercise, you have blessed everything — including making your own holy water.

Now take the holy water and pour it into one of the spray bottles. To the other spray bottle, add several drops of Eucalyptus oil, then add hot water. Take the salt and place it into a bowl before finally lighting the sage.

You are ready to start cleansing your home and reclaiming your living space. The first instruction I will give you is not to do the front or the back doors to your house or living space. These are to be left to the end and the last places to be done.

STEP ONE:

Go to your main living area and start in the first corner, moving from left to right as you go through the door. Drop a pinch of salt in each corner, then take the spray bottle with holy water and spray in the sign of your religion. For example, if you were brought up Christian or Catholic, spray the sign of a cross.

Move around the room and repeat this in each corner. When you are done, take the bottle of water and go to the window. Spray above all windows as you did in the corners, in the sign of your religion.

If there are any closets or cupboards, repeat in each one until the room has been cleansed with salt and water. Then go back to the door you came in and, same as you did above the window, spray the sign of your religion on both sides of the door. If there are any other doors in the room, do the same.

Proceed all the way around your home, repeating the process in each room as described until each room has been cleansed.

STEP TWO:

Take the lit sage and feather and go back around the house once more. With the feather, waft the smoke from the sage into all the corners and closets, going all around the living space. Repeat through the house until each room has been cleansed.

STEP THREE:

Put the safety glasses on and take the spray bottle with the Eucalyptus oil, this time going into each room. Start spraying toward the ceiling. Be careful around light fittings and spray the water all around each room. This will change the atmosphere bringing down all negativities.

> **Safety Warning:** Make sure you have unplugged electrical devices and cover anything that needs to be protected from water. DO NOT plug anything back in until it is dry.

STEP FOUR:

Pick up the bell or singing bowl and ring or play them in each corner of every room. Repeat this throughout the living space.

STEP FIVE:

Go to the rear or back door, open it, and place salt right across the threshold on the inside. Next, do the same on the outside.

STEP SIX:

At this point, you want control back in your living space. So go into each room, telling the negativity to get out of your living space. Don't leave any room or closet out. Take control back and remember this is your space, your house. Tell it to get out and mean it!

STEP SEVEN:

Go to the front door and place salt across the threshold on the inside, then do it on the outside.

STEP EIGHT:

Now that the clearing is done, close the door and shower or take a bath. Relax knowing you are in control of yourself and your home once more. This can be repeated the following week and, after that, as often as you want. Or you can just pick one of the above steps that you feel most comfortable with and use that each time you want to cleanse your home.

Again, I want to reinforce something very important before any energy clearings. **Never, ever start on the outside first!** You are going to cleanse from the inside out. If you do the outside first, you will be trapping any negativity inside. So again, we are cleaning from the inside to the outside.

CHAPTER 20:

ON BEING A MEDIUM

PART OF BEING a working medium is answering loads of questions. During readings, platform, or gallery sessions, I frequently get asked many questions, which has always been an integral part of my work. Over the years, I have made it my mission to learn and research my craft to answer these questions.

Over the years, the questions have gotten deeper and deeper, especially with my mediumship. As much as I understand the mechanics of what I do, I still struggle with *why me?* For many years, I thought this was a total intrusion into my life. The unbelievable anger and frustration I have encountered just to reach this point of my life is astonishing. Yet here I am, still trying to understand a small portion of what it is to be a human and what I do in life every day.

For a very long time, I considered speaking to Spirits a curse and, for the most part, hated this so-called gift! With a family, responsibilities, and a lack of a teacher, I felt that the "Spirit" was more of an intrusion and a curse than a gift. That's how I saw this work until a few years ago. I now see it as an ability that I have chosen to enhance the lives of others and, from time to time, expand my growth. I have studied hard in my life/career, and guess what? I still haven't got a clue as to what this is all about. As you can tell, I have remained very incredulous about it all.

As time passed, I realised I could help others through some of their darkest and lowest times. I have since agreed and understood with Spirit to try to work graciously side-by-side (good of me or what?).

It's about boundaries and has taken me a long time to understand. So, learn this lesson at the start: they (Spirit) will push and push until you say no, and you need to know to say no. They leave me alone at the end of the day or when I am done (called closing down), and I ignore them until I'm ready to work again. Learn that or you're no good to anyone. You will become tired and ill that way. It's not good for you mentally or health-wise if you constantly stay open. If you think you're missing something and have to stay open, then good luck with that!

Remember this if it helps: you are here to live your life. We need to stop being afraid to say no and mean it. We should put ourselves first from time to time instead of remembering everything we were taught as children: that you must help people. That you must be there for people and be kind. That is part of what we are here to do, to help each other, but not at our own cost! Just because we are spiritual doesn't mean we can't be selfish occasionally. It won't hurt to take time to be YOU, even for thirty minutes. If you can't help you, you won't be able to help anyone.

Chapter 21:

Final thoughts

WE ARE ALL entitled to look at mediumship and life how we want. NO ONE should ever discount anyone else's point of view just because they have made up their mind! I am just me; that's why Spirit wants to work with me, and they will do the same with you. It doesn't matter if you are the person who says, "Praise to the Lord, sweet Spirit!" or "Great Spirit, work with me." Or, like me, just "Go for it." Mavis Pattilla used to say, "It's your mediumship." She was correct; 99.9 percent of the time, I still consider her one of the best mediums ever. So, don't let your life as a medium be defined by anyone else. Listen and learn but make up your mind about the universe that flows around you.

Working with Spirit has its drawbacks which proper mediums or healers understand. Please remember that we play our part and Spirit plays theirs. You are a team working with love to prove to people that there is something so much more out there than this place.

Being a medium can be one of the most extraordinary things. It can also be one of the most frustrating, painful, and emotional ways to make a living. I've had good days and bad days. I have blamed everyone else, including God or whatever it is out there. And yes, throughout this book, you will see me talk about "God," like *love* or the *universe,* but I lost faith in whatever that is long ago, and I've learned not to be a *God-fearing* man anymore. I have every respect for what others believe and do, but that is not what this book is about.

I sometimes wonder what the elder statespeople in Spirit from this incredible movement who spent years developing their abilities would say about the way things are today. Rush, rush, rush. If this is you, and you are rushing, please remember to breathe. Let your life and mediumship evolve and mature as you nurture your relationship with yourself and your Spirit. And if you're serious about developing your mediumship, know it is a lifetime of work.

In the early years, life was not as quick, so people worked at their craft. People understood that this had to be structured and methodically worked. Today, we are surrounded by many distractions: television, radio, loud music, and, worse, technology (phones and computers!). We live life at such a fast pace, and no one wants to spend the time learning a craft that takes years to develop.

The reality of our world is sad; it's incredible to see the number of people who believe they are entitled to something without first putting in time and effort. Mediumship is not watching a television program about a working medium and then starting to give messages to anyone who will listen. It's about sitting around with other like-minded people, learning the finite details of whom you are first, and taking the time to understand the little stuff as well as the big.

All of this can benefit your growth, but racing down a road at 100 mph is useless if you can't control the vehicle and the wave of emotion that comes with it. The simple reason is that it stops your personal growth. In some cases, it will shut you down, and worse, you will burn yourself out.

The main reason this happens is that you haven't learned how to build and work with your energy! I have seen some potentially incredible mediums come and go over the years. But because they don't want to sit, learn, and take the time, they burn out and walk away.

Remember, Rome was not built in a day. Learn who you are in this beautiful energy and let it become a part of you. Gently enjoy the day-to-day stuff that can impact your life beautifully and lovingly. If I could say one thing about my growth, it is that it has never ended. Between us, me and my guides, we have always found ways to change things for me. Well, in truth, it is them, not 'us.' I ask for things and rarely get what I want. Instead, they find different ways to change it up.

I may not be explaining that the correct way, but for me, that's how it always seems. I don't believe I'll ever know anything about this. I know the basics, how much stuff works, and what it does with the people I help.

I'm a small cog in a giant wheel, and I've not even hit the ladder's first rung yet. (I'm trying to get as many metaphors as I can into this one paragraph.) I teach. I like to help, have conversations with people, do mentorship, and do readings.

I try to guide people as best as I can, but I certainly do not know everything. I know very little, but I have made it my mission to learn as much as possible to help others and make them feel confident with Spirit and their work.

However, the one thing that has done more to destroy my confidence over the years is the simple word NO. I have had to come to terms with the word 'no' to information supplied by Spirit through my mediumship, and it wrecks my confidence each time it happens. That in itself is something I am still learning about.

Just because the sitter says no, it doesn't mean to say the information is wrong. It could be the mere fact that they don't know it. The sitter may have to go and research. Maybe they were adopted and this is coming through from the family they have never known. They may have to recheck everything about who they are.

There have been so many times when I've had no after no and then received a phone call that I was right because they researched the information. Now, I'm not saying I'm perfect and right every time because I know I'm not. But if I could say one thing to encourage you, it's to keep learning.

When somebody does say no, understand that this is a learning moment in who you are and how you're going to let that affect your confidence. I have had to learn this the hard way. You need to know that you're not going to always be correct, and you're certainly not going to be wrong all the time. Know that your ego is now in play big time.

Do you smile, let it go, and carry on, asking them to check the information? Is it easy to just say, "Okay, if I'm wrong, all I can say is this is what I'm picking up from Spirit, and I'm sorry." If it continues, can you stand back and say, "I'm sorry, I'm not the medium for you," or do you continue to push this because you are never wrong — or you can't be wrong because Spirit won't let you be wrong? Do you think you are an incredible medium, the greatest medium since the dawn of time, and your ego is so big that you don't want to be embarrassed?

If you're not any of this, having an off day, and can let it go, please do it for the person sitting in front of you. They deserve better and need love and support.

Let me give you some advice on what I do. I always step away from all readings that go this way and explain that I cannot read for everyone. I'm not here to hurt anyone or make anything up or screw up somebody's first steps into having a reading because of my ego.

I promise you that this is going to test your confidence, your abilities, your belief in yourself, and your belief in Spirit. Some days I've done ten readings, nine of which have been spot on. I have done six that were great, then along came the seventh one that kept on saying no. So, I stopped and gave my reasons, then moved on to the final three, which were back to normal.

But at the end of the day, my brain has gone back to that one reading that didn't work. It is that one that has destroyed my confidence, and I will beat myself up something chronic. When Rob was alive, I would tell him about it, and he would go, "So you got 9 right? Was there any no's in the other nine?" My answer was no.

So, do you not think it is actually the person who is sitting down in front of you, who doesn't know the information and has to do research? Or is the person who has come and sat in front of you actually saying no because they have come with an ulterior motive, or they just do not like you and your personality has rubbed them the wrong way from the moment they have walked in?

As a medium, I can tell you somebody will always be worse or better than you. Just know the reasons why you do this work and understand what is happening on the day. Otherwise, you can end up like I have in the past, totally disillusioned and pissed off with the world and myself. There have been so many times in the past when I walked away from this at the end of the day so disillusioned by my belief in myself because somebody kept saying no. It's ridiculous how I allow my ego to beat me up.

I am still learning, and I am still trying to get confident. After all this time, I'm still trying to believe in myself and Spirit. So, remember, just know when you need to step back and let it go. Learn to allow them to walk away and find out the information, or help them find someone else, another reader. That's what I do, but that's just me. I want people to find their answers.

Part VII:

On Seeing A Medium

CHAPTER 22:

PATIENCE, SELF-TRUST & ENJOYING THE UNFOLDING PATH

THIS NEXT BIT COMES with a warning for everyone: *Please NEVER stop taking prescribed medicines unless advised by your medically licenced professional doctor or nurse.*

REPEAT: Never stop taking any kind of medication prescribed to you, and never stop going to the hospital or seeing doctors or nurses for treatments unless you have been discharged and no longer need them.

If anyone other than those professionals ever tell you in a spiritual healing session that you are healed and don't need to go back to these appointments, **report them immediately to their governing bodies.** Do not listen to them. They do not have the right to advise you that you are healed or cured.

And if you are a healer, never advise anyone to stop taking prescribed medicines. Please never tell anyone they are healed or cured, or that they no longer need anyone's help except yours. It is not for anyone other than fully licensed medical professionals to tell anyone to stop any kind of treatment.

Spiritual healing through Reiki should only be used as complementary to any kind of medication or help from a doctor, hospice, hospital, or nurse. It is NOT a replacement. I will repeat that: it is not a replacement for any medication or treatments received from medical health care professionals. They are *complementary* and meant to work along with your care from medical healthcare professionals.

When seeking help or treatment in whatever mode of healing, always ask for licenses, credentials, and how long they've been working. Ask them to explain everything thoroughly, including what will happen, the sensations, and whether you will feel anything hot or cold.

If they are going to touch you, ask them why they need to lay their hands on you. Remember, this is an intrusion into your personal space.

Your body is sacred to you. If they can't give you a response that satisfies you, walk away and find a practitioner to answer every question.

At this point, I could keep repeating the same thing. I have heard so many stories about people being hurt or ripped off for thousands of dollars or pounds. Sorry to go on and be so over the top, but everyone should feel comfortable and safe when seeking help.

When using any form of healing, there is never any need to place your hands on anyone. The healing flows all around, and as a vessel, we allow it to be directed to the client receiving it. At the end of the day, we all need to be protected from accusations or misunderstandings. Unless you are fully licensed to touch someone — i.e., a doctor, nurse, or massage therapist (and I mean the real deal, not the "Happy Ending" sort!), the list could go on here, but I think you understand — you should never lay your hands on anyone.

Spiritual healing can be one of the most beautiful things to experience. Using colour crystals and meditation is a great way to help clients. After, most will describe the sensation of feeling guides and loved ones around them.

I trained at my local Spiritualist Church, helping people to relax. I had to learn to allow the energy to move around and through me. I was just the vessel. It takes time and commitment to learn how energy moves. The healing energies are from God, the Spirit World, the universe, angels, or love itself. Take your pick.

The energy will work on rebalancing, calming, and relaxing you, and then it will start working at a deeper level. It is an energy coming forward from the light and will never discriminate in any way: not gender, colour, or religion. The concept of life force appears in most cultures, albeit under a different name. To the Chinese, it is *chi*. To Indian Hindus, it is *prana*. To Christians, it is *light*, just to name a few.

Spiritual healing has been a part of mankind for thousands of years through shamans, witches, witch doctors, the village's old lady, etc. In the last century, Harry Edwards was known for spiritual healing in the UK. He opened the "Harry Edwards Healing Sanctuary," in 1946 and held large public demonstrations throughout the UK. Edgar Cayce, an American psychic known as "The Sleeping Prophet" and the "Father of Holistic Medicine," would go into trance states to talk about healing and its uses.

In this vein, and as an understandable further precaution, as one braces to embark on their own spiritual unfolding with a medium, I am often asked, "Will spirits ask me to do bad things?" This needs to be addressed as a medium. We are often asked to help people understand about being possessed, and if Spirit would ever ask you to harm someone?

The answer is NO, NEVER!

If you believe that Spirit is telling you to do this, seek medical assistance immediately. You may have a medical condition. Please stop, do not do anything, and seek help from fully licensed medical professionals before seeking out mediums and psychics. We should only assist you by directing you to professional medical help.

Everyone who passes over is offered love, light, and help in the Spirit World—no matter what they have done here. But there are Spirits that, for one reason or another, will refuse to go into heaven (the Spirit World) and stay earthbound. These are lost and interfering Spirits that have refused to move into the light and can become *attachments*. If this is the case, you are not picking up beings of light from the Spirit World.

Again, if you are or know someone who is hearing voices and they are asking you to hurt others, please seek out professional medical help immediately.

I OFTEN GET people who will come to a reading and ask, "What do you see about my health?" This is a tough one to answer as a reader, even though I have been doing this work for many years. It's something that I refuse to answer for the simple reason that I'm not a doctor or trained medical professional. My advice is again to *please seek medical advice*. I will repeat the same statement in every reading: "I'm not a doctor. If you are worried or concerned about your health, seek help. I am a medium, not a health practitioner."

There are mediums and psychics who will answer this, but the problem I have is that everything we pick up about people is not always going to be correct. I can fill this book with horror stories about mediums and psychics who have frightened the crap out of people with diagnoses, only for the sitter to go to the doctor and surprise, surprise, nothing is wrong with them.

Some health-intuitive workers are medically trained doctors and specialise in their work as doctors and intuitives. The reality for the rest of us is simple. We have doctors because they are licensed to work and diagnose health.

Okay, good, now that that's out of the way... how do you get the best reading from a medium or psychic?

WHEN BOOKING A reading with a medium or psychic, as with anything in life, do yourself a big favour: research, research, and research some more. A reading is a very personal thing. It can be enlightening, frightening, and annoying. If you don't get what you want, research further.

Ensure you understand what you want to find out or what you need to know. Are you looking for someone who has passed into the Spirit world? Seek a medium. Alternatively, do you want to look into the future? Is it your love life you need to sort out, or are you at a junction where you don't know which turn to take or what to do? In this case, seek a psychic.

After researching what reading will suit you best, go back to researching. Take time to look at your reader. Ask your friends, check the internet, and continue your research. Sorry, but it's the only way to go. After you've researched and decided which way to go, what now?

Your job as a sitter is to make the medium work. You are NOT there to give them the answers. It is their job to provide you with information. Do not answer direct questions like, "Is your mother or father dead?" or "Do you know anyone in the Spirit World?" If someone claims to be a medium, they must be able to give you evidence without asking questions.

Never feed the medium with your information until the reading is over—and only then if you need to! They should be able to give you a description of your loved one.

If you are the reader and the sitter does not understand any of the information within the first 10 minutes of reading (and after confirming the information back with Spirit, and it is still a no), explain that you are sorry and stop reading. Do not let your ego get involved. Let it go. The person sitting in front of you is not ready.

Working as a medium is like playing charades. Sometimes we get things the wrong way around. There may be times when the medium cannot work; they may be having a bad day and unable to do the reading for you. This is not down to you or them. Sometimes it doesn't work for one reason or another.

Lastly, remember that psychic or medium readings should not become a crutch or an addiction. Our souls came to this Earthly plane to experience and co-create our lives. Do not disempower yourself by allowing others to make your final choices. Your free will makes you unique, so don't give your power away—even to a medium or psychic. When deeper healing or guidance is needed, that's where a trusted therapist can truly support you.

WE EACH EXPERIENCE the loss of a loved one differently. The depth of mourning is very different for every one of us. Seeking help to deal with your grief is paramount.

We will see people in the first few months following a death, but after that one visit, I advise someone not to do this again for at least a year. We all have to move on, and in every case, we encourage people to find a way to grieve and live once more. That is the message I have always received from Spirit. Mourning the loss of a loved one is probably the hardest thing we will ever go through in life, especially if it's a child or a parent at a young age.

We each mourn differently and for different lengths of time. Having trained as a counsellor and coach, I understand that in some cases, the profound extent of the mourning period may indicate that a person needs professional help and will direct them with advice.

There are times when mediums can help with the loss of a child, a murder, or an accident. We all need closure after a sudden death without the chance to say goodbye. In these circumstances, mediums can provide a vital service and evidence to help people come to terms with death.

I have seen people who are still mourning the loss of someone twenty, thirty, and forty years later, such as was my case until I got counselling in the UK with Margret and Tony Slater and Cruse Bereavement Counselling. I was forty-seven—precisely forty years after my mother passed when I finally dealt with my grief. I had therapy over the years, but it was after my brother Nicky and best friend Cyril passed, and then I lost a relationship with Manj that I finally stopped blaming myself for my mum's death.

Speaking from my own experience, this question has lingered in the quiet spaces of my life, and I've done my best to meet it with honesty. But grief doesn't follow a timeline, and it certainly doesn't come with instructions. It's different for everyone. Trying to define it is like trying to measure a piece of string that keeps changing shape. Some days it stretches endlessly; other days, it coils tightly around your heart. What I've come to understand is that this journey isn't about finding the perfect answer—it's about learning how to live with the questions. And even when the path feels uncertain, know this: you are not alone, and healing has a way of finding us, even in the quietest moments.

There are numerous counselling services in the USA and UK. If you require help, please only seek out qualified professionals and research them properly. Additionally, if you are not happy with the service you are receiving, stop and explain to the counsellor or therapist why you are leaving, then start the search again. With any counselling, you must feel safe and supported.

People often come to me looking to contact their spouses who have passed away, hoping to get a message of love. Most mediums will tell you that just because you come to see us for a reading doesn't mean anyone you were hoping to talk to will show up and you'll get what you want. It doesn't always work how we want or expect.

When getting a reading, sometimes your great Aunt Glad or Uncle Phil will come through first to provide guidance, simply because they may have gone through something similar when they were in the body and understand what is happening to you with your emotions. Remember, they are also from your team of guides/helpers and will have been around you since they passed over.

At first, the medium may not be picking up the one you hoped would come through. If they were quiet, withdrawn, shy, or super polite, they may sit back until last, no matter what we want. If that's how they were in the body, that's how they're going to be in Spirit. They will let others communicate through us first. It is down to the Spirit to come forward, not for us to decide who goes first!

I have stopped readings because the person sitting in front of me kept saying no, that was so-and-so, but I wanted someone else. I understand this frustration, but if you are going for a reading, it's not good being fixated on one person. There are so many loved ones trying to help you live again.

There could be several reasons our significant others don't come through for a while. It may be down to that person adjusting to the other side, or maybe you are not moving on and living your life. They will wait for you as long as it takes. They won't give up but will wait for you to help you first. So, I'm going back to what I said earlier: please seek therapy first, then consult a medium only when you have started to come to terms with your healing.

I can tell you that when a reading doesn't work, the medium will be just as disappointed as the sitter. There have been numerous occasions when it hasn't worked, and I can tell you I have blamed myself and been exceptionally cruel to myself for days. I doubted myself, the voices, and Spirit. Then everyone in my team of guides and helpers from Spirit told me the same: it wasn't time for them to get a reading, and I wasn't the medium to help them now. I can tell you that when it doesn't work for me, I don't charge. I apologise and try to explain.

I would like to add that over the years, I have been lucky with some of the teachers I have had in my progress as a medium. In a class with Sandie Baker at AFC, she gave me a different way to talk to someone from Spirit. If all else fails in a reading, I ask for the name of the person they wish to contact and try to make contact that way. This does not always work, and if it doesn't, I can only apologise and continue to talk with the others or finish the reading.

IN CLOSING OUR little orientation here, one more thing I am regularly asked is, "Can a medium or psychic give me the lottery numbers?" The number of times a day we are asked this one! Sorry, but the answer is NO. Okay, some may try and be sort of successful. They may claim they can and, if they can, then good luck to them.

The question is, though, why don't they win it every week? And if they did, would they want to be talking to the likes of you and me?

Having said that, if someone out there can give us the lottery numbers, please feel free to do so! You can get in touch with us just by visiting our website, www.KitandNatalie.com, and sending us an email with the winning numbers! ☺

CHAPTER 23:

GRIEF

"The way we regard death is critical to the way we experience life. When your fear of death changes, the way you live your life changes."[x]

—RAM DASS

VISITING A MEDIUM after the death of someone is down to the person you are as you try to deal with carrying on living and facing each day. The loss of someone impacts us all in so many different ways. I can promise you that every death is unique, and the way we mourn is distinctively down to who we are. It all comes down to the way we love, the way we care, and how we choose to live again for ourselves.

Having been a medium and doing this work for so long, if I could say one thing to help you understand as you move through your grief, it would be that Spirit, particularly your loved one, wants you to know they are always with you. They want you to feel safe and secure, knowing they have passed into love or the light and are always there. They will encourage you to take this time to heal.

Know that as you mourn and heal while trying to remember the good and bad, you have begun one of the most arduous journeys back to love for you. When finding your way to the truth of who you are, this road is strewn with love, hurt, pain, and sometimes hate. This is *your* road, and it's down to where you want to take it—and there's no time limit. You must feel safe and loved again, but from the inside.

Ignore others' views or opinions on how to grieve. Feel every bit of it and permit yourself to do this the way you want to, not the way others tell you.

One of the most important things I learned as I went through my grieving was to recognise that I was entitled to feel all the pain and hurt. But more than that, to acknowledge the anger inside of me for those losses. And I was doing it for the first time after nearly thirty years of hurting myself and anyone who got in my way. Near enough, everyone will go through a loss of some kind throughout life, and we each face it in our own immutable way.

People will often say to you in a time of grief, "I'm sorry. At least they are not in pain," or "You will get over it." We tell each other it will be fine. However, with this approach, even though it's said to have love attached to it, it does not reflect how you feel inside and isn't helpful.

The pain may have stopped for my loved one, but it won't stop *my* hurt because it is here twenty-four, seven. Eventually, people stop saying things, but the problem now is they are avoiding you. God forbid anybody know that you're in pain and struggling to face each day. I mean, what the fuck! Who wants to see that?

In some societies, people do want to see it. They know that it's healthy to mourn and want to engage, but not ours here in the West. It's great for a while. They want to talk and let you know you have a shoulder to cry on. Then, because our loss is so personal, others get to the point of not knowing what to say, not knowing how to behave, and not knowing how to treat you. I don't understand. In a caring and loving society, why should we care if somebody sees us mourning? We shouldn't!

But now it's like you have a deadly disease and must be avoided at all times, just in case you're going to give that mourning disease to them. In today's society, people don't want to see others in pain because it makes them uncomfortable. Everybody should be happy, and something is wrong with you if you're not.

When we're being avoided, we get this from people: "Hi, oh, I'm sorry I'm having a crazy day, we must talk soon." "Sorry, I've got to get home for the kids." "Sorry, I've got a work thing." It goes on and on.

It's so important that you understand this: We all have a right to feel every emotion, including anger, frustration, emptiness, and all of that, fuck your feelings of abandonment. We are left to face each day without that special relationship that we shared and the love we gave each other every day.

One of the worst things that happened to me was that I started fighting myself. At every moment, my head would never shut up. I constantly felt like crap, and I was always beating myself up for feeling this way. WTF!

Probably at this moment, your head is going around and around as you try to get by day by day and understand a world that can't stop as everyone else carries on with their lives. You could be feeling lost and locked in this hurt, wondering why your loved one left you here to face life without them. This is *grief*, and you have every right to feel every ounce of that meaningless death.

They may have given us life or meaning. Whether they were grandparents, mothers, fathers, brothers, sisters, children, friends, lovers, husbands, wives, or even pets, they gave us an experience of truth in our hearts. It's at these points we have to truly remember: love yourself. Hold yourself in love and trust.

I would love to tell everyone that when you lose someone, everything is going to be all right. But the reality is I have no right to say that, no matter what my belief is about where my loved ones are. *I* know they are safe and well. On the other hand, when I work as a medium, I offer love and support with evidence from *your* loved ones.

Hopefully, I prove that they survived the death of the body. But, and it's a big "but," *you* have to come to terms with this loss. Know this is a time for you to recentre yourself to find your peace. Losing someone can be incredibly hard, but sometimes it's life's way of reminding us that we're still here for a reason. That's why this will be the most challenging part of the journey into you. But remember that each step forward is about you and your healing.

I have constantly gone through death. I've lost so many people in my life. It's a constant theme. I'm a medium and grief coach, and that's what I do. However, the death of my friend and teacher Rob shook me to my core. I couldn't work for months because of my total anger and loss. It has taken me quite a few years to get used to the fact that he's not here in the body. I can't call him, text him, or email him. I have gone to do this so many times, and then I realise he's dead.

You may think that as a medium, I would understand all these things, and my answer would be, I do. But when it comes to me, I don't. I can be great with other people, but with my pain, I'm crap at dealing with it.

I suppose when you look at it, it's life. But I was recently doing my grief coaching course, and I realised how much it still was affecting me. With the help of everybody in the course and Pat Sheveland, I started to move through some of my stuff again. This may be a theme, and it may be part of my life; but it sucks, and I hate it.

Rob still comes around. I don't get to laugh and joke with him, even though he still sits in the car with me occasionally as I'm driving around the state working. It's just not the same. I am so grateful for him being in my life and pushing me to do my work. But the one thing I miss the most is his friendship. It meant more than words can describe.

As I wrote this section, then rewrote and edited it, I thought, *Is this me putting another spin on things?* I don't have a right to say that, and I'm genuinely not advocating that you see a medium. My strongest advice is to encourage you to seek professional help. Find a grief therapist. Find a counsellor. Find someone you can trust to talk to about all of this.

What I can tell you is that visiting a medium has helped me find myself and move forward. Again, I keep returning to this one thing: death is so different for each of us. Along with that, our beliefs are so different, and that's great because if beliefs were the same, we would be robots—worse, with a limited emotional understanding of each other.

As I've developed my abilities through the years, I have seen some amazing mediums work and some incredulous egos hurting people with personal stuff said on a platform/stage. A warning for all mediums: when someone shows up at your office, there could be a million different reasons they have turned up at your door, been brought to a church or a community centre to see you. Mainly, the Spirit has brought these people to see you, and you need to remember that for those few minutes. They deserve respect and to be treated with kindness.

These souls are lost, lonely, and mourning. You are dealing with someone who, in their mind, feels that they have failed to save someone close to their heart. They may or may not have been with their loved ones right up to the end and witnessed loved ones go through the most incredible pain.

The person sitting in front of you may have been watching their loved ones go through this for years, with everyone wanting and hoping to find a cure, but it didn't come. Their loved one could have died in the most horrendous way: an accident, rape, or murder. Now, because someone they truly loved has passed away, they may have given up on life themselves.

Does it hurt to treat them all with dignity on both sides, here and in Spirit? The answer is NO. So please think hard about who you are. Think about why you became a medium, what you are doing, and why you're doing it. And if you can't do it respectfully, stop doing it!

Mediumship is not about cramming a message down someone's throat in a church, hall, auditorium, or standing on a platform. It's not about getting people's stuff out in front of a crowd and going on and on until the person gives up because you think you are brilliant and correct in everything you're saying.

If you must be like that, then I'm sorry. You are doing the wrong work. You need to get another career! People's lives are not there to be put on show, so someone at the back of the room thinks you're incredible. Please stop making us all look crazy. You are being intrusive to someone who has come to receive healing because they are grieving. We have been given mediumship to heal, not abuse.

Do the reading with the same love that you would want when getting a reading yourself. Consider how you would like to be told and work accordingly. And if you want to help all of your clients, take a course on grief coaching. Not a weekend one. Spend some time learning something precious to you.

As I wrote, rewrote, and edited this chapter, coming back to it time after time—and even as I read it now—it feels repetitive and drawn out. But for me, it's not.

I found a bit more peace as I used this opportunity to spill out my frustrations repeatedly, so I've left everything in. I hope this helps you understand that you are you, and you're loved from the other side. We all are individuals, and as we go through this pain and let the world go about its day, I'm going to acknowledge that I'm in pain and I'm going to feel it *for me*.

One of the saddest things that happens in a reading is working with parents who are coming to terms with the loss of a baby or child. I can tell you that it is not an easy thing to navigate as a medium.

As with any death, it is painful. But these souls are at their lowest point in life and have reached out to their friends, risking being judged by their belief systems and families. They have come to you as a reader to help them understand this particular death.

Know that some may have crossed the boundaries of their religion in the total belief in life before this death. They have specifically come looking for you because they want closure and need to know that their baby has returned to their God. I want you to understand that you are being given the most incredible privilege to help the parents find peace and live again.

Through all my years of dealing with this issue, I have the conviction to stand by my belief that every child or baby that comes to this place leaves knowing where it is returning to. They are received back into the light by angels and pure love. The important thing for everyone to understand about the moment they leave is that it doesn't matter how they pass—whether that be a miscarriage, abortion, suicide, or an accident.

Every one of us knows before we come here; we will understand whether it is staying on this planet to grow or just to experience life within another body. It is an experience we all go through in the evolution of our souls because it is a massive learning point in our understanding of every part of life and death.

Please, please, please understand that if your child has passed into the light, whether it be by miscarriage, abortion, suicide, or accident, that child has gone back safely to the other side. There is no guilt, no pain. Your child is happy on the other side growing up and is grateful for the experience and the love you shared with them for brief moments in your body or life.

CHAPTER 24:

A CHAPTER ON PETS

Can my pets come through in a mediumship reading?

YES, AND THEY frequently do. I have described countless pets to their owners in readings. It's not one of my strong points, but on a trip to Arthur Findley College (AFC) a few years ago, we met a lady who contacts pets' Spirits. Her name is Gina Lorraine Murray, so we asked her what her experiences were, and the following is in her words:

> My mum was very much into rescuing animals, since before I was born. We had cats, dogs, and rabbits, along with wild birds, hedgehogs, and even a swan

that lived a fair bit of her first few months indoors as she was imprinted on my mum. So, I already had a bond with animals from an early age.

It was when I was ten that I had a very vivid dream about animals on the other side, in the same place as everyone else... not a separate "kingdom" as so many books and mediums try to say. I remember the following day telling my mum all about it, and from then on, I knew I would see all my wonderful animals again.

Over the years, my sensitivity, mediumship, and healing grew. I worked in various alternative therapies—massage, reflexology, healing, colonic hydrotherapy, etc., during the day. However, I continued following my spiritual and mediumistic pathway during this time.

One medium, many years ago came to me and said there were many animals around me, thanking me for their healing, and that was it. I tended to notice at meetings and demonstrations that the medium may say, "There's a cat beside you," but that was about it. I was also getting many friends and relatives commenting and asking questions about their beloved pets who had passed over, and over the years have had grief-stricken pet owners say that they have been told they will never see their animals again.

I studied animal communication, and it was whilst healing a horse that I realised the way she was communicating with me was the same feeling as mediumship. I have since had many experiences of mediumship with my animals, so over the years, I have worked on this aspect.

I see the animals, feel them, and express their love and memories, like I do with mediumship with people. I often have people come to me for reading purely to hear what their animal friend is like. Many have stronger links with animals than with people, and often, there can be much guilt if a pet has had to be put down.

Pets are often far wiser than any relative that comes through! I was doing a reading recently for a young man and his dog came through, much to his surprise and delight. The dog was telling me what was going on in this man's life. After the reading, the man told me that his dog had been his closest and most trusted companion.

Whilst on a course a couple of years ago in a mediumship class, an Alsatian came through before the human! When the class ended, the tutor told me that I should focus on people and get the person first. It turned out that the recipient of the reading was pleased to hear from their dog.

The week I got home, I had a lady come in for a reading. I couldn't see anyone with her, so I carried on chatting and, in the end, had to tell her about her dog and two horses with her. It turned out she only wanted to hear from them!

During readings, a much-loved pet will pop in to say hi. It is often the animals that bring great emotion. They work in the same way as people do—with intense feelings and emotions, they will impress on your body's physical sensations, love, and sadness. They put images and even words in your mind, and I don't mean barks, squeaks, etc.

Where there is a bond of love, they stay. They will be waiting to meet the person or persons they have shared their life with on the other side, just like our loved ones.

I could go on and on here, but in all the years I have worked as a medium, I feel strongly that this is an aspect of mediumship that has been overlooked. If you would like any more information, then you can go to my website: www.ginalmurray.com.

We asked Gina to answer this question as she has a better understanding than we do. As I have said in this book, it would not be for us all to be the same! To us, this is just another fantastic way of working with Spirit.

And yes, *animals have Spirit guides,* and they are much nicer and more helpful than the human-looking ones. In my experience, they will come in to offer strength, guard, guide, and protect. They can be former pets in this life or a previous one (if you believe in past lives!). Or one of our other central working guides will feel that, at a specific moment, we need the reassurance of an animal to give us something that cannot be gained from a human-looking one.

Animals are also psychic, and anyone who has ever had a pet will understand this answer. They can be the most loving and loyal friends, for no reason other than that's what they want to do. Stories worldwide tell of pets saving people's lives with their incredible gifts of foresight.

How many times a day do you watch them looking into a corner of the room behind you or sitting looking at the chair where their owner sat? I recently did a reading for a lovely lady whose father had recently passed, and when I walked in, I was greeted by two old dogs. They looked at me, instantly started looking behind me, and then both sat down at my feet, looking at me throughout the reading. At the end of the reading, the lady told me they were his dogs and was not surprised they sat with me.

I think the hard thing for us as humans to understand is that pets, along with all of the animal kingdoms, have their journeys in this world and the next.

"All beasts, as well as our pets on your planet, are usually much more in alignment with their inner being than most humans."

—ESTHER AND JERRY HICKS,
*The Astonishing Power of Emotions:
Let Your Feelings be Your Guide*

We love our pets as much as the next person. Our cats are The Ginger Boxer (named by our granddaughter Nicole), Ollie (who was named by our other granddaughter, Jasmine), and Principessa—which is *Princess* in Italian—who was named after I watched the film *A Life is Beautiful*. And now we also have Newt, named after Newt Scamander.

I can tell you they're far more spiritual than I will ever be and know exactly who they are. I am well-trained by everyone, and I love it. They are the most perfect beings of love, ever.

Note: *I'd like to thank Gina here for all her insight. She's an incredible animal communicator and, when it's my turn to speak to her—which is obviously never going to happen because my pets are staying here with me and God can sod off; he's not having them back because they're my children now—I just want to say, thank you so much, Gina.*

Conclusion:

The Art of Life

"When the faith is strong enough, it is sufficient just to be. It's a journey towards simplicity, towards quietness, towards a kind of joy that is not in time. It's a journey that has taken us from primary identification with our body and our psyche, on to an identification with God, and ultimately beyond identification."[xi]

—RAM DASS

THE ENERGY I connect with to communicate with your loved ones is available to everyone—not just a select few. It belongs to us all. It's the universe's way of saying, *trust in me and I'll help you be you. I'll help you find your path, get your goals, and find your peace.* You don't have to believe in anything other than you. All the universe longs to do is guide us toward peace and help us truly live in harmony with our soul's purpose.

I see people every day trying to find a way through the bullshit they have been told by life or society. It's like they're not good enough to do anything else. Whether it's in readings or people coming to a class, I see lots of them having to face the reality of life. They stay in place because of this irrational fear that someone out there is correct.

Society has instilled fear in us from little children. This is how I eventually told myself to get things for myself. I simply said, "Screw it. I'm entitled to live. I'm here for a reason, not for anyone but me to decide!"

"You are loved just for being who you are, just for existing. You don't have to do anything to earn it. Your shortcomings, your lack of self-esteem, physical perfection, or social and economic success – none of that matters. No one can take this love away from you, and it will always be here."

—RAM DASS

Working in this universal energy, light, or love amazes me. (I'm having a good day as I write this!) Working as a medium with people has become an integral part of my life. It doesn't matter what you call it. This love is there for us all to blend with, and we can all receive the gift of truth from whomever your God is. I am asked constantly about the bullshit that is politics and religion and what is happening to the world just lately. Well, I have been giving this answer to everyone: God does not pick sides. He/She is concerned about all of us. Each of us is here to heal and help one another. Stop allowing this negativity to live rent-free in your mind and do the work you came here to do. Please remember to live your life, not the one you believe God or spirit is judging you for. You have free will to live a life that makes you happy.

As I continue my life, I still struggle, like most, to understand the journey. In truth, I have a sneaky suspicion that this is all we can ever do in the grand old scheme of things. However, there is so much more happening to and around us at a soul level. We have all been given access to a playground, to be open, and to discover so much more than our brains can grasp in this plane of existence. But if we occasionally allow our entire being to breathe and cease thinking solely with our brains, we might just catch a glimpse of the truth of who we are. When we take the opportunity to peek, when we step outside the boundaries we have created to keep ourselves in place, we allow the universe to reveal some of its truth and beauty, and the chance to grow beyond this body is bestowed upon us.

As for me and my view, since becoming a past-life regression therapist, the universe has presented a new path, new adventure, and an avenue of research for me. It has not allowed me to see everything I want to see, but it is providing me with an opportunity to expand my knowledge. So, from originally not wanting to write anything else, I now have two more books in the works. In one of them, I intend to discuss how I feel there is currently *something else* happening to us all, which I am sure will land me in an asylum very quickly.

As you move forward in life, please remember that *you're incredible.* We all have an extraordinarily vast amount of energy called love around us, and not one life form or being is refused that healing. It doesn't matter what your religion is. It doesn't matter what you look like or what you believe in. It does not matter. This energy has been provided by the universe/God for us all to tap into and gain knowledge daily to grow into whoever we have decided to be in this lifetime. Just open your mind to it. Don't let anyone tell you that you cannot do this because you can. If you're here on this planet, you're here to learn. If you're learning, you can access this pure love.

When it's all done, you don't have to come back here again for any more lessons over the million lives we have to live. (*Oh my God,* I HOPE IT'S NOT THAT MANY!) The journey will continue in another way because we are trying to get back to love itself. I believe there is life and love above the Spirit World, and as souls, we are trying to obtain that truth too; there can't just be here, there, and it's done.

Please take note of this because YOU are here to live this life and do what you want. If you want to be a medium psychic or healer, do it. Do it if you want to be a vet, teacher, or mountain climber. It doesn't matter how old you are or what's wrong with your body. Get out and live.

The universe is beyond anything our tiny brains will ever absorb. Something awaits us. The easiest way to describe it is to say that *love waits for us all*. It's all-knowing, and everyone is surrounded and held in it. It's not some older man with a white beard wearing an old white cloak. It's just love. This is my truth and belief, and it's what gets me through the day and has for a long time. The vastness of love is always there waiting for us, always supporting every single one of us.

I have found life to be fun, painful, and, at times, a bloody nightmare. This book is about the answers I sorted out myself, having reached the tender age of 65. These are my truths. There are a lot of teachers, books, and other experts in their fields who know a lot more than I do, and some who do not. Some fantastic things have happened to me, and I have met some remarkable people. But what's important is that *you* start searching for what's important in *your* heart, defining you as a medium and a person in your own right.

I have made many friends and had some engaging experiences while trying to grow into a relatively decent human being. I believe that probably not everyone would agree with that statement, and I have a few exes who would not think that at all! But what can I say? I'm here, still learning each day.

One of the great things about life on this planet is that we all get to make a choice and are allowed to pursue our own reality. That's what we should be encouraging our kids to do. Find the greatness in yourself, and you will find the greatness in this world.

The reality is that if you have a great teacher who encourages you to explore and find other teachers, I'm pleased. If anyone out there is telling you that they are speaking the truth for God or Spirits and that they know everything, then ask them why they are still here if they already know all there is to know. Every teacher should always encourage you to explore who you are. My favourite line from Mavis Pattilla was, "This is your mediumship," and she was so right. Please remember that.

The reality of why I wrote this was just to prove something to myself. I'm just a little cog in the wheel of life. Spirit loves me, and they know how much I love them. "I'm me." Please just be you because with all your faults, you are beautiful, and Spirit wants to work with you.

Then there are the new pioneers of Spiritualism, people like you. We are all moving forward with an understanding of life after death, thanks to the great mediums and teachers who have given their time and, in some cases, their lives. Through the years, they have spent energy and time reaching out to the next world or universe for the truth about who we are and what is next. As much as people work in this movement today, there will never be the same amount of effort that was put in over the years, mainly because everyone wants to be a medium NOW!

"The art of life is to stay wide open and be vulnerable, yet at the same time to sit with the mystery and the awe and with the unbearable pain— to just be with it all."

—Excerpt from *Polishing the Mirror: How to Live from Your Spiritual Heart* by Ram Dass

ACKNOWLEDGEMENTS

I WOULD LIKE to thank each of the following for helping me become a better person, medium, and teacher, and for inspiring me to find answers.

I couldn't have done this without John (my primary guide), my mother, and my inspiration to all of my loved ones in Spirit — my grandfather, grandmothers, and friends.

I'd also like to thank anybody who's ever come for a reading, and all your loved ones who came through to prove that I'm a medium on a good day. Without everybody's support, I wouldn't be here to this day. It would have ended in some strange way long ago. Rob Brown, my friend and mentor, (I miss you every day), Natalie, Mum, Dad, Nova, and Simon.

Judith, my friend, I owe you, my life. I'm breathing and sober because of the love you shared, and I'm here because of your constant support. There is a quote from The Shawshank Redemption: "Get busy living or get busy dying." Because of you, Judith, I got busy living. I love you more than you will ever know.

I am deeply grateful to Mrs. Heather of the Learn Write Centre in Long Eaton. Her unwavering support and encouragement were instrumental in my writing journey. Without her, none of this would have ever been written.

Thank you to Trudy, Cyril, Evelyn Carrington, Ida Harrison, Mavis Pattilla, Olive Haynes, Robert Brown (Nottingham), Josie Hancock, Sandra Dunne, Colin Bates, Sandie Baker and Angie Morris. They have all inspired and helped me find answers.

I have stayed in touch with Pat, my colleague and mentor. It's her fault that I teach; she guided me in doing it at Charnwood Spiritualist Church in Derby. As I mentioned, we met for the first time in 1983 and still meet every time I'm in the UK. Coffee and cake are always the order of the day. We reminisce about our original teachers and how they helped us become the mediums and teachers we are today. Without them we would still be lost or, more than likely, dead!

And Pat's sister Yvonne (the mouthy one!). They are now running their own Spiritual Centres called "Flows Angels" and were always trying to get me to do things.

I have been blessed with friends who tried to get me to move forward.

And if it had not been for Manj, I would not have been doing this work because she kept me going. So, thank you Manj, and you Rob and Pat, for believing in me and giving all your support.

Susan Duval, who was a great help in my early days of working in the USA, and for introducing us to Eric Anzalone, from the TV show "What Matters Most."

Over the years, I have been fortunate to receive help, encouragement, and guidance from numerous individuals. While it's impossible to mention everyone by name, I want to express my heartfelt thanks to each of you. Your support has been invaluable, and I apologise if your name is not mentioned here.

There have been so many others who have been there while I tried to write this book through my dyslexia, and they were so patient with me: Natalie, Ami, Terri, Taylor, Lindsey, Denise and now Christine who has got me to the end. I think they all either broke down or nearly killed me. And we'd like to thank Rodney Miles for, as he puts it, "developmental editing," but I call it "sorting out my shit."

I would also like to thank the following:

Pam Owen

Margaret Slater and Anthony E Hartwell

Ami Manning

Gina Lorraine Murray

Relate UK and University of East London

Grief Coach with Pat Sheveland and B.R.E.A.T.H.E.

Charnwood St Spiritualist Church Derby

Doris Stokes

Audrey Norris

Arthur Findlay Collage

Margret Allen (medium Derbyshire)

Mother Teresa

Garre Liana

Dave Allen, comedian

Margaret Fishback, Powers Footsteps

Patricia Seaver McGivern

School of Hypnotherapy Tampa

Harry Edwards Healing Sanctuary

And other religions that have influenced my beliefs and work, including Christians, Catholics, Judaism, Sikhs, Muslims, Hinduism, Buddhism, Spiritualism, and Zoroastrian

Many listed above are sadly no longer with us and have all passed to the Spirit World.

In closing, THANK YOU ALL for the love, support, and kindness I still receive from everyone.

ABOUT THE AUTHOR(S)

Image © 2025 by the Author (selfie!) of Kit Mitchell and wife Natalie

FOR OVER 25 years, Kit has served as a practicing medium, offering heartfelt connections between individuals and their loved ones in the spirit world. His mediumship work is rooted in compassion and a deep respect for the spiritual journey, often providing comfort, closure, and insight to those seeking answers beyond the physical realm.

In the last few years, Kit has trained as a clinical hypnotherapist. His professional journey led him to the Institute of Interpersonal Hypnotherapy in Tampa, Florida, where he completed a 500-hour program in Hypnotherapy, Clinical Hypnotherapy, and Transpersonal Hypnotherapy. These studies deepened his understanding of the subconscious mind and laid the foundation for his work in past life regression and spiritually centered healing.

Integrating his intuitive gifts with hypnotherapy Kit helps clients explore their inner worlds, uncover past-life patterns, and live more authentic, empowered lives. His practice is inspired by the belief that healing is both a personal and spiritual journey—one that begins with self-awareness and leads to profound transformation. Along with the above he is a certified life, grief, and couples coach with a lifelong dedication to healing and personal revolution. Born and raised in England, he has spent decades supporting individuals through recovery, grief, and many challenges in life.

LEARN MORE / START YOUR JOURNEY

Discover Your True Self and Inner Peace
with Mediumship Readings, Hypnotherapy and/or Coaching

Welcome to a transformative journey with an experienced medium, certified practitioner of clinical hypnotherapy, past life regression, and grief, couples and life coaching. My mission is to help you uncover your authentic path and achieve lasting inner peace. Whether you wish to delve into your past lives, gain profound insights into your present self, or heal from grief, I am here to guide you with expertise and compassion. Specializing in past life regression and grief coaching, I offer tailored sessions designed to unlock healing and personal growth.

Don't wait to start your journey towards a brighter, more fulfilling future. Reach out today to schedule your session and discover the path to healing. Visit us online today!

www.KitandNatalie.com

And connect with us on Facebook!

https://www.facebook.com/KitandNatalie/

FURTHER STUDY

FILM & TV

It's a Wonderful Life (film) 1946.

Parenthood (film) directed by Ron Howard, 1989.

Life Is Beautiful (film) by Roberto Benigni, 1997.

The Invention of Lying (film) by Ricky Gervais, 2009.

Quantum Leap (television series) 2017.

Becoming Nobody (documentary about Ram Dass), 2019.

PEOPLE

Andrew Jackson Davis, with the basis of philosophy and foundations of Modern Spiritualism.

René Descartes, French philosopher and scientist.

Edgar Cayce, the "Sleeping Prophet" and "Father of Holistic Medicine."

PUBLICATIONS

The Astonishing Power of Emotions: Let Your Feelings be Your Guide, by Esther and Jerry Hicks with Abraham.

Conversations with God, Neil Donald Walsh.

Soul Rescuers: A 21st Century Guide to the Spirit World, Terry and Natalia O'Sullivan.

Michael Newton, PhD, *Journey of Souls, Destiny of Souls*, and *Wisdom of Souls*.

Brian Weiss, M.D., *Only Love is Real, Many Lives, Many Masters*, and *Same Soul, Many Bodies*.

John Bradshaw, *Homecoming: Reclaiming and Healing Your Inner Child*.

Radical Compassion by Tara Brach.

Layer Cake by J.J. Connolly.

Rita Hayworth and Shawshank Redemption, a novella by Stephen King.

The Essential Ram Dass Collection, 2019, and anything by Ram Dass.

Jack Kornfield, and everything he ever wrote or talked about, he was such an inspiration to peace, including his works: *Awakening Is Real, The Buddha Is Still Teaching*, and *The Jewel of Liberation*.

Robert Owen, social reformer, and *The Rational Quarterly Review*.

Fantastic Beast and Where to Find Them by Newt Scamander and J.K. Rowling.

Carl Jung's Theory of Personality: Archetypes & Collective Unconscious by Saul McLeod PhD.

Death and Life by Dolores Cannon,

WEBSITES

Thanos. *Wikipedia* - www.en.wikipedia.org/wiki/Thanos

Minister Steven Upton, Public Relations Officer, and The Spiritualists' National Union website: www.snu.org.uk.

Notes

[i] https://www.ramdass.org/ram-dass-quotes/

[ii] "Poll: Most Believe In Psychic Phenomena" by Bootie Cosgrove-Mather. April 29, 2002. —https://www.cbsnews.com/news/poll-most-believe-in-psychic-phenomena/#:~:text=Even%20though%20an%20equal%20number,4%25%20of%20non%2Dbelievers.

[iii] "How Common are Psychic Moments? 1 in 3 Americans Feel They Have Experienced One" by Yael Bame. October 31, 2017. —https://today.yougov.com/entertainment/articles/19534-1-3-americans-feel-they-have-experienced-psychic-m

[iv] "Everyone can have psychic ability—mediums are rarer" by Bonnie Page, "Ask the Psychic Medium," *Sentinel and Enterprise*. February 6, 2018. Updated July 11, 2019 —https://www.sentinelandenterprise.com/2018/02/06/everyone-can-have-psychic-ability-mediums-are-rarer/#:~:text=Also%2C%20being%20a%20medium%20and,state%20about%20a%20certain%20situation.

[v] "The Weirdest Facts We Never Knew About The Psychic And Medium Industry" by Diana Price. *Ranker*. Updated September 8, 2022. —https://www.ranker.com/list/weird-fun-facts-about-psychic-industry/diana-price

[vi] ibid

[vii] https://medium.com/change-your-mind/higher-self-do-you-have-one-d3457db1a3aa. Accessed 2025-12-20.

[viii] https://www.encyclopedia.com/religion/legal-and-political-magazines/summerland#:~:text=Summerland%20is%20a%20Spiritualist%20term,tradition%20have%20informed%20the%20Summerland.

[ix] https://www.quora.com/What-are-some-mind-blowing-facts-about-mediums

[x] Copyright © 2025 Pumpkin Limited

[xi] https://www.ramdass.org/ram-dass-quotes/